*j*ulia bourland

the go-girl guide to the first year of marriage

*h*ITCHED

atria *books*

new york   london   sydney
toronto   singapore

ATRIA
BOOKS

First Atria Books trade paperback edition 2003

ATRIA is a trademark of Simon & Schuster, Inc.

For information regarding special discounts for
bulk purchases, please contact
Simon & Schuster Special Sales at 1-800-456-6798
or business@simonandschuster.com

DESIGNED BY ELINA D. NUDELMAN

Manufactured in the United States of America

1   3   5   7   9   10   8   6   4   2

Library of Congress Cataloging-in-Publication Data
Bourland, Julia.
Hitched : the go girl guide to the first year of marriage /
Julia Bourland. —1st Atria Books trade pbk. ed.
    p. cm.
1. Marriage. 2. Wives—Life skills guides.
3. Weddings—Planning. I. Title.

HQ734.B745   2003
306.81—dc21   2002043796

ISBN 0-7434-4410-8

for **lawrence**

$\mathcal{A}$cknowledgments

Obviously, this book would be hogwash, to borrow a phrase from my Texan heritage, without the inspiration, support, and wisdom gained from my partner in crime in marriage, Lawrence, who also just happens to be my personal hero. I adore you a thousand times over.

I am very grateful to my agent, Alicka Pistek, who has always supported my career goals and decisions, risky though some may have been. For your careful negotiations and professional persistence, I salute you.

Thank you to Greer Kessel Hendricks for recognizing that the saturated market of marriage books failed to reach one critical demographic: smart, progressive women. Because of your fantastic editorial insight on year one and on marriage in general, newlyweds of the millennium owe this read to you.

This book would be nothing without the thoughtful reflection and introspection on marriage of the sixty hitched women (all of whose names and some revealing details have been changed to ensure privacy) and the many experts I interviewed over the course of writing. Thank you all for opening your minds and hearts to me, giving me a rare glimpse into the private lives of married women. Your accumulated expertise on marriage has given this book the depth I never could have achieved on my own.

Finally, I want to thank Sue Pierce and Audrey Wong for their valuable feedback, and family and friends who have excused my social isolation over the past year due to The Book. Thanks for understanding.

Contents

$\mathcal{P}$reface

Before there is a wife, there is a fiancée. Before there's a fiancée, there's a girlfriend. Before a girlfriend, there is a single woman looking for love. (And before her there's a single woman who's not looking for love, but she predates the premise of this book.) Since this is where my story begins, it's only fair that I brief you on how my husband, Lawrence, and I met. Besides, I love telling this story.

I was walking to work, over five years ago, taking a route I rarely took because it led me up and down one enormous hill after another, and when you live in San Francisco, you try to avoid the hills (although one look at my calf muscles would show you how feeble that attempt can be). But for unknown reasons—fate?—I had wanted a change of scenery, so I began the forty-five-minute hike to my downtown office early one morning.

At a stoplight a man came up beside me and said hi. I glanced at him, probably scowled as I often do to strangers, and muttered something closely resembling "hello." Then I looked straight ahead, hoping the light would change so I wouldn't have to talk to some guy who was trying to pick me up before my morning coffee.

The light turned green, and I launched into my signature sprint-walk. It turned out that this guy had a sprint-walk, too. He asked if I was heading to work. I told him yes and asked if he was doing the same. Yep. I considered crossing the street but didn't want to appear rude. He was cute.

"Where do you work?" he asked. I didn't respond right away. Instead, I did a quick mental assessment: Could he be a mass murderer who would perpetually harass me if he found out where I spent my days? He *did* work downtown, which I illogically rationalized mass murderers did not do. I told him the name of the magazine where I was an editor, then asked what he did.

"Architectural engineer." This provoked a titillating discussion about what architectural engineers actually do, as well as the various buildings he was in the process of engineering. One of his recent projects was an environmentally sustainable bank in Frankfurt. He was intelligent. And when his projects took him to construction sites, he wore a hard hat. Mmmm.

Our conversation then drifted to the various articles I was writing and editing at the magazine; one was a controversial piece on circumcision. "Yes or no?" I demanded his views. He smiled instead of feigning agony, as most men do when the subject of circumcision arises (though it rarely does in normal conversation, I admit). His irreverent and somewhat mysterious response to my query was intriguing.

We walked and talked until our routes diverged. Then I forgot about him. Months passed until I ran into him again on my way to work, walking a different route. This time we exchanged numbers and began a late-summer friendship filled with movies, hikes, bicycle rides, and an occasional lunch. We were dating by Thanksgiving.

At the start of the new year a strange twist of fate sent us both to New York City with our jobs (though I like to think that he followed me there), and it was in Manhattan that we fell irreversibly in love. But even after that year of East Coast seasons, we were far from ready to get hitched. It took our moving back to San Francisco and three years of living together before we made that move.

Why I Wrote This Book

The first time Lawrence and I discussed marriage explicitly (as opposed to making coy insinuations about wanting to spend the rest of our lives together) was at a seedy bar in the Mission, the *über*-hip, *über*-urban district of San Francisco that's slowly becoming gentrified because of couples like us who order fancy cocktails inside its seedy bars. I brought it up.

"Are all your friends and family asking you when we're going to get engaged? Mine are," I stated a little more aggressively than I had meant to. He grinned and said no. We sipped our martinis.

"Well, all of my friends are asking me when we're going to tie the knot," I said into my drink. "Have you ever thought about wanting to get married?"

We had been living together for more than a year, but neither of us had ever muttered the M word. I was beginning to wonder why. Besides, we had just been to the wedding of a girlfriend of mine, and all my friends were throwing hints that we were next. I wanted to know for sure.

"Well," he began cautiously, "*would* you marry me?"

I froze. Was Lawrence proposing to me? Was this *it*? My proposal story—my mind raced—was going to be that my boyfriend asked me to marry him *inside a dark seedy bar in the Mission!* I couldn't breathe.

Not that I didn't want to marry Lawrence. The truth is,

I was ready to make my commitment—in three months, after I had turned in the final draft of my first book, *The Go-Girl Guide: Surviving Your 20s with Savvy, Soul, and Style.* I didn't want an engagement to distract me from my deadline. Likewise, I didn't want my deadline to distract me from my engagement.

"Are you asking?" I practically stuttered.

We sat smiling nervously and clutching each other's hands, clammy from surprise at the way our conversation had turned. Minutes passed before Lawrence broke the silence: "Actually, I had never imagined asking you to marry me inside a bar."

Thank God! We both relaxed and giddily told each other that we wanted to get married—eventually. We talked about where we'd want to have the ceremony (in the Bay Area), what type of wedding we'd want (spiritual, not religious), and where we'd like to honeymoon (somewhere adventurous and warm—New Zealand, perhaps).

During the months that followed, I threw myself into finishing my book, and neither of us brought up the topic of marriage again. Even after I had turned in the final draft of my manuscript. Even during the highly anticipated (and grossly overrated) millennium New Year's Eve, which followed shortly thereafter. Even when Valentine's Day the following year came and went. By spring I was exasperated, and that surprised me.

I had never been the type of girl to obsess about the way my future husband would propose or about getting married. Nor had I been the type to fantasize about my wedding day. And, for the record, I'm not the type who's ballsy enough to do the proposing myself, though I have the utmost respect for women who are. But the longer those pre-engagement months of anticipation were drawn out (due to the enormity of this lifelong decision, I found out later from my cautious husband), the more anxious I became to make our commitment official. I wanted our devotion out in the open and celebrated. I wanted to throw a fancy party for all our family and friends to mark the occasion. But most of all I wanted to stop obsessing about the whole thing.

Then, on April Fool's Day (you have to wonder about the timing), it happened: During a Saturday afternoon hike, while sitting side-by-side on a clearing that overlooked the Pacific Ocean, Lawrence held my hands and asked me to be his wife. We were on the same trail we had taken years before when we started dating. Having replayed this moment on more occasions than I care to admit (but never quite as romantically or emotionally as the real thing), I said yes within a beat. Actually, I think I first laughed obnoxiously and said "Ha, ha, April fool," but never mind the details. The proposal was earnest, and we hit the jewelry stores that afternoon.

Those of you flipping through this book who are newly engaged can probably relate to the bombardment of emotions, from euphoria to fear to confusion, that hits you like a Mack truck the moment you and your mate decide to spend the rest of your lives together. What you might not know (but what those of you who are in the thick of your first year of marriage are well aware of) is that this chaotic state of mind lasts well beyond the engagement days.

On that formidable April Fool's Day, I was completely unprepared for how the engagement, wedding, and first year of marriage would change my life. After all, Lawrence and I had been living together for so long, what would possibly change by uttering those two simple words: "I do"? The answer: everything (and in the best possible ways). But

I didn't know that then, and, frankly, I had my concerns.

Would I succumb to the stereotype and alienate myself from my single girlfriends? Why did all my free-speaking gal pals suddenly turn tight-lipped about their sex lives after getting married? Would I still be able to write a beautiful novel someday while simultaneously nurturing a sexually charged relationship with a man who buys box after box of experimental cereal that sits in our cupboard for months before I secretly toss it out?

And then there are the daunting statistics: Both Lawrence and I come from families of divorce (–2 points). We lived together for three years before we exchanged vows (–4 points if you believe those studies which claim that living together before marriage predicts divorce). We've never had to deal with major trauma in our relationship, giving us only an inkling as to how we'd combat future slings and arrows (–3 points). And we probably have unresolved childhood issues to burden our bliss (–1 point).

Married women rarely share details about their transformation from single to hitched, so in many ways the passage into marriage is a solitary initiation. Sure, you have an army of enthusiastic bridesmaids to help you dicker with the details of wedding planning. And many of you can consult a friend or two who has already made the leap of faith. Surely your female power team (mom, sisters, best girlfriend) can offer some support during the first year of marriage.

But really you're on your own when your mate turns his back on you in bed and says he's not in the mood. Or when you and your husband enter round three of the "saving for a vacation to Beijing versus buying an exotic rug for the living room" debate. Those are the times when marriage can feel isolating and lonely and, above all, cause a confusing mix of emotions, even in the most confident and independent thinkers among us. That's why I wrote this book.

Hitched is the guide that will prepare you for all the changes that await you during the first year of marriage. It will warn you, for instance, that friends, family, strangers, and the tax code view you differently as a married gal. That the first thing many women do when they find out you're married is glance down at your ring finger (what, for proof?). That some people will think being married is an oddity. A hitched girlfriend of mine was once at a cocktail party, talking to friends of friends. They asked her if she had come with anyone, to which she replied, "My husband." They were in shock. "You're married?!" they gasped. It was incomprehensible to them that a married couple would go to a party where singles mingled, let alone separate upon arrival, dress as stylishly as they did, and have interesting things to talk about.

To get perspective on year one, I interviewed sixty straight-talking women who had recently tied the knot. Most of these women were college educated, liberal, and living in urban areas. Many were recommended to me by friends and colleagues who knew I was seeking interviews for this book, and most of the interviews were conducted over the phone. Our conversations ranged from how they shared money with their mates to how often they had sex to how they resolved their most bitter conflicts—topics so personal that I'd be hesitant to broach them with some of my married girlfriends! To protect these women's privacy, I have changed their names and some personal details. When expert advice was in order, I interviewed marriage counselors, family therapists, sex coaches, and financial advisors. Our cumulative wisdom and experience will offer much-needed advice and shed light on life with a husband.

For the record, I have no clarity on life with a same-sex domestic partner and therefore have left out specific issues pertaining to lesbian couples who have devoted their lives to a partner. However, I hope that much of what is in *Hitched* will translate into a myriad of different "marriages," since making a lifelong commitment to another triggers far more relationship issues than those specific to sexual orientation.

In *Hitched* I will reveal the many unspoken details about this life-altering year and provide you with fuel to make the most of it. I will give you the inside scoop on all the changes that are going to take place in your friendships, your career, your sexuality, and your financial goals. I'll share with you savvy advice on dealing with your changing looks (yes, your looks *will* change) as well as how to carve out your own sense of space. I'll prepare you for the best and the not-so-best milestones you'll face during year one of marriage, starting with the engagement. I might even make you laugh about it all. Shall we begin?

$\mathcal{M}$entally engaged

The marriage initiation begins with an engagement. And an engagement, regardless of whether the proposal was over-the-top romantic, spontaneous (which is also romantic), or heavily anticipated, typically conjures up a hurricane of emotions—enough to make a girl downright weepy when giving her best friend the blow-by-blow playback of the proposal, or downright bitchy when she finds out that the reception site she really wants is booked until 2010. Discussions with your mate about various wedding details will keep this hurricane of emotions active (but, hopefully, not too destructive) throughout your engagement.

Planning a wedding tends to bring out a couple's feelings about everything: money, religion, family, tradition. It's one life event that touches on every macro issue out there. Even if you consider yourself a low-key kind of gal, you may be surprised at the degree of passion you feel about every little detail that goes into your wedding. I certainly was. But what might be helpful to note is that this whirl of emotions is a normal mental state typical of many women about to enter the unknown alternative lifestyle of marriage. What follows is a list containing some of the feelings you might have during those engagement months when you and your mate realize that your lives are about to change forever.

dazed and confused

One of the first sensations many women feel after getting engaged is dazed. Lori, 34, of San Francisco, California, felt this spaced-out phenomenon immediately after her boyfriend popped the question (also on a hike overlooking the Pacific Ocean—a popular engagement spot here in northern California).

They had bushwhacked to a secluded area. Hopping around and nervously fussing over everything they had brought, from the picnic to the binoculars, Lori had a gut feeling that the proposal was moments away (she had actually felt the outline of an engagement ring in her boyfriend's pocket on the way up the hill), and all her emotions were on the verge of eruption.

When her boyfriend took her hands and asked her to be his wife, she was instantaneously propelled into a daze. The emotional intensity was too much, she says, and she totally shut down. The best she could manage to utter in response was "Yeah, okay." Of course it wasn't long before shock turned to giddiness (thanks in part to the champagne her boyfriend had brought along to celebrate), but the dazed mode returned not too long after when her fiancé called his family to share the news.

Faith, 29, of Los Angeles, California, felt a similar shock when calling family members to share the news of her engagement, which happened while she and her mate were stuck in traffic on their way to Ikea. (His proposal wins the creative award, by the way. He asked her by suggesting they play the game of Jeopardy: "The answer is yes." Faith then guessed the question: "Will you marry me?" So, technically, she asked him.) But when they told relatives, she was bombarded with unexpected inquiries: "Are you pregnant?"

(No, she wasn't.) "Are you going to share finances?" (The thought had not occurred to her.) "Are you going to change your name?" (She had no clue.) She felt invaded and irritated, primarily because she hadn't worked out all these things in her head and wanted her engagement to be more of a private time between her and her fiancé.

Important note: The dazed sensation will likely return again and again throughout your engagement, so get comfortable with it. Being in a state of shock is a natural response to the emotional overload that initiations such as weddings breed. Of course, the daze won't always be associated with shock. Some of it will come in the form of simple daydreaming. Rarely in life will you experience as many daydreams as when you're planning a wedding.

My dazed state of mind tended to hit me on my way to work, when I was sitting in traffic, disparaged by the long string of cars in front and behind me. There, I dreamed about the wedding ceremony—our readings (spiritual and evocative), our vows (standard contemporary), the kiss (soulful), the music (harp soloist, playing Bach), my dress (a backless, biased-cut, 1930-style silk white gown), and my hair (help me!). Such daydreaming had a calming effect, especially when I was feeling particularly stressed about wedding planning. I suppose therapists would call this mental phenomenon "visualizing," but I'm (hopefully) over my therapy days, and daydreaming has a more romantic sound to it, don't you think?

Part of this spaced-out phenomenon may serve as a mental response to another common state of mind experienced by many brides-to-be during their engagement: confusion. I hope your confusion is not about your choice of husband. If it is, I suggest you calmly discuss your decision to get married with a therapist who will help you distinguish the irrational doubts and the internal devil-dialogue that accompanies all wedding-related panic ("How can I marry a man who won't initiate any of the wedding planning tasks, obviously indicating that he won't be a good father?") from real doubts about your fiancé's character or his ability to communicate or work out problems.

In most cases, confusion has to do with the tremendously overwhelming task of planning a fabulous and emotionally loaded party for your nearest and dearest, people you feel irrationally compelled to dazzle with your tasteful and graceful entertaining skills. Confusion will likely aim to damage brain cells not long after getting engaged, when your family and friends begin the barrage of questions on matters you likely haven't even begun to consider: When's the date? Where will it be? Who are your bridesmaids? When are you going to try on wedding dresses ("because, you know, you'd better start looking *right this minute*")?

Isabelle, 30, of Chicago, Illinois, had a mother who was particularly bent on adding to the wedding planning chaos. Her mom called her nonstop to ask if she had decided on invitations, chosen a band or DJ, did this or did that, all the while reminding her that the clock was ticking and she'd better get on top of all the tasks pronto! Near the end of all the planning, Isabelle could barely speak to her mother without yelling and then either slamming down the phone or running away from her (literally).

This might be an appropriate spot to mention the effectively proven mantra of wedding planning: When faced with questions that are stressing you out, the best response is to repeat over and over again: "I don't know." Admit that you don't have opinions about certain details, then change the subject. This may drive the traditionalists among your clan of supporters crazy, but eventually they will get bored and move on to sharing their opinions about the way you should conduct your wedding. When you get bored, it's time to focus on non-wedding-related conversation (if you and your tribespeople can remember what that's like).

Part of the reason confusion is rampant is that the wedding initiation carries with it a wagon-load of etiquette that most of us are completely ignorant of, having performed only occasional acts of gratitude since leaving home, such as writing thank-you notes to grandparents after receiving birthday checks. From the proposal on, there are so many etiquette details with which to contend: Whom to invite? Guests for single friends: yes or no? Which of your closest friends and dearest relatives should be attendants? And how to tell your other close friends and relatives that they are not?

Next, there are all the gritty, tedious details that must be dealt with when you're planning a wedding, most of which involve well-timed coordination. For instance, you must immediately book the wedding if your heart is set on a particular date, especially if that date happens to fall during high wedding season (April to November). This is particularly difficult if you've never considered the type of wedding you'd like. What's more, that date must work for all your VIPs (parents, wedding party, favorite relatives, and best friends). Then there's the matter of booking a honeymoon (another immediate task if your wedding falls within high tourist season), not to mention all the wedding ceremony details, starting with the kind of ceremony you want to have.

I'm not going to sugarcoat the wedding organization confusion, because chaos is part of the mental preparation needed to take you through the marital rite of passage. Get a good book on wedding planning (there are millions of them out there; take your pick depending on how modern or how Martha you want to go), then let your instincts call the shots. And keep this in mind: The rewards you receive from throwing a big party, during which all your favorite people in the world will surround you and exude shock-waves of love and support and compliments on this momentous occasion, are worth every minute of it.

princessy

Many women feel uncharacteristically princessy upon getting engaged, possibly due to all the attention brides-to-be typically receive when they announce their marital intentions. Even the self-described jocks and the no-nonsense among us get caught up to some degree in the fanfare. There aren't too many occasions in life when that princess feeling will hit you so poignantly as when you're engaged, so embrace it now, ladies.

The inner-princess state of mind often overcomes you when you call your parents, siblings, and best friends to tell them the exciting news of your pending union. In most instances they will all emit joyful gasps and coos and offer eloquent and supportive commentary on what an amazing couple you and your husband-to-be make. These moments often help calm some of the other less desirable feelings that an engagement also breeds (more on these in a minute). And for those relatives and friends who don't praise your wonderful choice of mate, promise yourself not to include them again during your wedding planning efforts. They will only help to push you off your gilded cloud.

Another common occasion during which the princess feeling hits is when you and your fiancé shop for an engagement ring if you and your mate choose to get one or if he hasn't already surprised you with one. Salesclerks will give you their well-worn "aren't you two adorable" look and compliment you and your intended on everything from your exquisite taste in rare and precious jewels to the delicacy of your hands and your recent manicure. And even though the salespeople's ultimate motive is to sell a ring, I believe their enthusiasm is genuine because, like most of us, they adore an engaged couple, which represents optimism and passion in so many people's minds.

Once you choose an engagement ring (or slip on the one that your husband picked out on his own), another bizarre phenomenon often occurs: Everyone begins to view you differently. When Lawrence and I got engaged, we waited a week before purchasing my engagement ring, a pale blue sapphire set in white gold (by the way, many women love describing their marital jewels and relaying any related history or relevant details). For unknown reasons I wanted to obsess over my choice, hitting practically every jewelry store in the Bay Area to check out my options. When I told people about my engagement, the first thing they did was look down at my ring finger for proof. When they saw no evidence, they averted their glance immediately. Once I got the ring, though, it always drew comment (as will any engagement ring on any woman's finger). The world, especially the female population, loves an engagement ring.

Those of you who choose not to wear an engagement ring, due to a lack of funds or due to principle (the principle being that a bride-to-be shouldn't have to wear a symbol that marks her "taken" status, a throwback to when women were considered the legal property of men), will also note the strange power an engagement ring has in our society. Those without a ring may notice that others appear disappointed or even skeptical about your commitment to your fiancé (or, more pointedly, his commitment to you). And then there's always the gossip ignited by a sparkling new engagement ring. Rarely do men make assumptions based on such rings except whether or not to waste a pickup line, but women often comment behind a new bride-to-be's back about the size, weight, and style of her engagement ring. Some even make such comments as "He must really love her to have given her that hunk of a diamond." I hate such comments, by the way, but now I'm getting way off the point of that princessy feeling, so let's get over the jewels.

Another time you may truly feel like a royal kind of gal is when trying on wedding dresses. Even if you're planning to borrow a dress or browse through the ball gown racks at vintage clothing stores for the retro-bridal look, scheduling appointments at bridal boutiques is one ritual not to be missed. When else are you ever going to get to prance around in front of a gorgeously lit mirror wearing exquisite silks, tulle, and organza? And when else will salespeople treat you so kindly? And when else will you get to try on veils and tiaras that really do make you look regal?

Besides, this is often the first time you will get stares and smiles from rubbernecking strangers who are peeking in the boutique windows as you twist and twirl, pose and shimmy in front of the mirror, checking out every angle of yourself in a dress. All brides-to-be trying on wedding dresses are stunning, and this is when you'll catch yourself exuding that premarital glow. If you are seriously shopping for a wedding dress, here's a word of advice: Take your most stylish and honest friend with you so she can tell you truthfully which dresses make you look like the ballerina in your first jewelry box, which make you look like Ginger Grant of *Gilligan's Island* (my likely subconscious influence), and which make you look like the unique and stunning bride you were destined to be. The truth is, you may be so completely mesmerized by the rare and exotic fabrics of the bridal gowns that your sense of style may be temporarily malfunctioning—in a kind of way that years down the line when flipping through your wedding album you'll exclaim, "Oh my God, what was I thinking!"

unworthy

Along with all the regal attention they receive upon getting engaged, many brides-to-be experience a parallel feeling of humility. The humility may start with the engagement ring, especially if this is the first expensive piece of jewelry you've ever owned, not to mention the most costly present your mate has ever given you. Funny how such a small (albeit expensive) offering can simultaneously induce palm-sweating excitement and a flash of undeserving guilt—especially if you know how badly your fiancé wants a new road bike. Trust me: Guilt usually passes pretty quickly, but it may return due to other events.

The congratulatory hugs and phone calls, the celebratory cards from family and friends, the engagement and bachelorette parties, and all the gifts—the attention directed toward a newly engaged woman is enough to make any girl feel humble if not downright guilty about being the source of all the fuss. This humility may continue through your wedding day, especially if you're the type of girl who begins trembling uncontrollably at the thought of hoarding everyone's attention during the celebratory vow-swapping ritual. For many women the engagement is one of the most sentimental periods in their life, and feeling overwhelmed by all the sentiment comes with the territory.

But here's the shocker: You may begin to like this attention during the course of your engagement, because humility often transforms into other feelings, such as gratitude and appreciation for your great friends and family. By your wedding day, humility may even have been transformed into exhilaration, not unlike that of a rock star surrounded by the paparazzi of family and friends, armed with cameras, all wanting your attention.

For those especially prone to guilt: Don't let humility rob you of your natural right to celebrate this rite of passage. One woman I interviewed, feeling particularly guilty for having so much attention lavished upon her, chose not to invite all her friends to a bridal shower thrown by her mother-in-law-to-be, because she didn't want her friends to feel that they had to go to yet another party for her or buy her yet another gift. Her friends' feelings were hurt as a result. The truth is that most people in this world love to celebrate weddings and the fanfare that surrounds them. Allow them (and yourself) that pleasure.

fatalistic

Judging from my research, fatalistic thoughts are another common feeling experienced by many brides-to-be during the marriage initiation. As with daydreaming, mine always hit during my commute. As I sat in traffic, I imagined horrific scenarios that might prevent my upcoming union. One recurring doomsday vision was my little black Beetle flipping over the side of the San Mateo Bridge. Dara, 27, of Tampa, Florida, also had fatalistic thoughts during the months leading up to her wedding, but hers involved a plane. She would think of the tragedy in terms of headlines: ENGAGED COUPLE DIES IN PLANE CRASH.

While fatalistic thoughts may just be a product of stress about the upcoming initiation, my admittedly unscientific theory on the matter stems from the idea that marriage is a rebirth—one that involves ending our life as a single woman and beginning a new life with our husband.

I'm no psychologist, but it seems that when one is entering a rebirth of sorts, a part of our psyche needs to die (or at least drastically transform). So perhaps these fatalistic thoughts are the part of our psyche that's acting out its final death scene in the form of car wrecks and plane crashes. The good news is that these fatalistic images are just that— your imagination working overtime. Avoid fixating on them. You have enough to contend with without planning the end of the world, too.

bitchy

Another common (and, might I add, less desirable) emotional side effect of getting engaged is a wave of bitchiness. One positive aspect of this uncharacteristic behavior is that friends who know you well will often excuse your attitude, chalking it up to stress.

My bitchiness, sadly, was often directed toward my undeserving fiancé and appeared in the form of nagging, a trait that up until I got engaged had escaped my repertoire of unflattering personality disorders. I began to initiate bitchy arguments with Lawrence over various wedding disagreements: the ceremony and reception venue (I wanted a city wedding, he fell in love with a castlelike venue across the bay); honeymoon planning (who would plan it and when); the guest list (when he would put his list of addresses together so we could send out invitations).

Based on some of the interviews I've had with other

hitched women, it seems that snarls are not uncommon during the engagement. Lori experienced one blowout with her fiancé just days before the wedding. As with many hitched women, she can't recall exactly what that fight was about, but she does remember that in the heat of the moment she suggested calling off the wedding because of it. Luckily, her fiancé was savvy enough to understand what was really going on: engagement stress. He calmly told her to grow up, upon which she burst into tears (a good stress releaser).

One thing to keep in mind: Fights with your intended are synonymous with wedding planning. That lesser-known fact goes against the grain of wedding-related romanticism, but most brides-to-be, if they are honest, can admit to one or two prenuptial moments they'd prefer to keep in the closet. Money is a common source of bitchiness. You'll likely be spending more than you want on this momentous occasion, and if you and your fiancé are paying for the bash yourselves, there will be tension if, say, one of you wants a traditional wedding bouquet (and we all know who that would be), and the other thinks he can pick up something cheaper for you at the corner flower shop the morning of.

Isabelle, who has now been married for three years, recalls how money-related angst affected her attitude toward her fiancé. It wasn't long into her planning that she realized her Cinderella dream wedding was way out of her budgetary reach, and she'd have to settle for, as she put it, the blue-collar version. As a result, she was moody, irritable, and unable to deal with her fiancé throughout most of her engagement, leaving her amazed that they even ended up getting hitched. A self-proclaimed perfectionist, Isabelle took on all the wedding planning tasks—even the items traditionally left up to the man, such as the rehearsal dinner and honeymoon—which added to her stress and, therefore, the relationship's stress.

Parents and in-laws are another common source of conflict for many engaged couples, because many of them come with their own expectations for the wedding. Dara got into a fight with her fiancé over their reception planning, which his parents began to micromanage not long after their engagement. The short story: His parents wanted them to throw a 700-person finger-food bash so they could invite all their friends and their second cousins' kids; Dara's parents had in mind a more intimate 200-person sit-down dinner. When her future mother-in-law mailed the couple her proposed astronomical guest list, it started a silent World War III. Dara, not wanting to be a difficult daughter-in-law (but desiring even less a sandwich reception for 700 people she didn't know), had to ask her fiancé several times to rein in his parents' robust enthusiasm for their guest list so the couple of honor could have the more intimate sit-down reception they dreamed of. Eventually the two clans were able to come to a compromise, but not without some fierce discussions, one of which prompted Dara's fiancé to suggest calling off the wedding—but only for a brief moment of stress-induced misjudgment.

Another common source of contention among many a bride- and groom-to-be has to do with their conflicting opinions about the ceremony and/or reception details. While it seems that brides-to-be often have more opinions on such items as favors for the guests, china patterns, and the wording on the invitations, I've discovered in my interviews that when it comes to making final decisions on certain things, many fiancés suddenly have strong opinions, too. Lori's fiancé, for instance, chose to voice his opinion that the wording on their Save the Date letters was awkward while he and Lori were licking the envelopes shut. Lori's roommate, who was helping with this task, kindly told him to back off! After all, if he cared so much about wording, he could have initiated the task of writing and mailing the cards himself. But, typically, guys don't initiate wedding planning tasks, which is a whole other issue, really.

Other times this conflict revolves around religion, especially when the betrothed come from different religious or cultural backgrounds or from families who will expect the wedding ceremony to follow a certain tradition or faith, even if it's not the one that the couple personally endorses. Since cultural tradition and religion may not have come up in their relationship prior to organizing a wedding ceremony, this often stumps many couples. This part of wedding planning is often loaded with childhood memories, family expectations, or even your own spiritual beliefs. We'll talk more about this in the next chapter, but for now just keep in mind that it's a common source of stress in prenuptial planning.

This brings me to the final thing I'm going to say about this topic: Bitchiness is a by-product of stress. Take the time leading up to your wedding to practice your favorite stress-reduction tactics. If you've never established them before now, here are a few to get you started: Get plenty of exercise (thirty minutes a day, every day, and increasing the intensity the more stressed you become). Eat well (translation: no more M&Ms for lunch). Drink plenty of fluids (and I mean water, not Diet Coke). Get regular bouts of sleep, meaning go to bed and wake up at the same time every day. If you can afford the time off, plan a weekend away for you and your mate about a month before the ceremony, when planning stress is often at its peak. Promise yourselves that you won't discuss wedding planning the entire time you're away. The point is to reconnect, not argue.

hungry

If you're like most brides-to-be, almost as soon as you and your mate decide to get hitched, you will embark on Mission Impossible: to lose ten pounds before W-Day. The typical result is that you will be hungry during your entire engagement, especially if you're planning a short engagement.

Why so many of us are obsessed with looking fit and trim in our gorgeous white (or otherwise) gowns is a sad commentary on our female psyches, but what else is new? I admit I did the dieting and exercise routine for three solid months before my wedding day. I was hungry and cranky and pissed off about the fact that after all my years of battling the body image demons, I still based a little too much of my identity on the way I looked. Plus, it didn't help that I had gone to Italy not long before the countdown began and came back laden with so much pasta weight that my wedding dress was what you'd call a tight squeeze.

I did manage to drop five pounds by religiously pounding the treadmill after work every day and cutting out fatty snacks (that alone cut my daily caloric intake in half) and limiting my meals to one serving only. One problem with pre-wedding dieting is that your level of hunger is often directly proportional to your level of bitchiness. It's best to avoid both. But if you do partake of this pre-wedding female ritual, do so responsibly by focusing on exercise, not by substituting normal meals with diet drinks or experimenting with the latest diet *du jour*.

terrified

Clearly, not every bride-to-be feels doubtful or downright fearful about her decision to get married, but I heard it enough in my interviewing to warrant a brief mention. Some of you may wonder whether you've made the right decision in your choice of lifelong mate. Others may fear that you're not the marrying type of gal. Or that your current lifestyle is going to be so dramatically altered, mutated, or even violated by the institution of matrimony that you, your dreams, and possibly your own voice will all but shrivel up and disappear. To add to this fear, you've started daydreaming—even fantasizing—about ex-boyfriends. One woman I interviewed even reread old love letters from ex-boyfriends that she kept in a shoebox, wondering how she could possibly make this love work when others had failed. Adding to your fear is the very traumatic act of wedding planning. All the decisions you and your mate will likely be arguing over (politely, in some cases, and raunchily in others) throughout the bloated months leading up to the big day will very often serve to validate or reinforce your doubts.

Rest assured, many of these feelings of terror are completely normal and most likely are due to the unknowns brought about by change, not to mention the stress you're under (even if you're the type to deny that you're under stress when you're half-buried in it. Many of the happily married women I interviewed for this book felt the same way—even as they were walking down the aisle, in some cases. Let me add that this fear is a mighty force to contend with as you and your mate plan your lifelong future together. Unchallenged, it may serve to undermine all your decisions about marriage and steal some of the joy that's rightfully deserved during this unique time.

If you feel doubt, trepidation, and uncertainty about your decision to tie the knot, there are a couple of things you can do to determine if this is pre-wedding jitters or a warning sign that you'd better postpone the wedding until you feel more certain about taking the leap. First, determine whether your doubts about your husband involve fear for your safety or well-being. If there is even a hint that your husband-to-be is violent, excessively controlling, or has the potential to be abusive, DO NOT GET MARRIED! Postpone the date and sign yourself up for couples therapy. Marriage does not cure abuse.

If your physical and emotional safety isn't at stake, the next step is to talk to your girlfriends about your doubts—especially those who are married and have been through this formidable passage. They know you and your relationship fears, as well as what may be a product of pre-wedding freakout. A long talk may help you figure out what's driving your doubt. If you're worried about deep-seated conflict between you and your intended (conflict you may have discovered as you began to plan the wedding, when talk of family, finances, and even religion are part of your daily discussions instead of the usual courtship conversations of work, friendships, and what you're going to do on your next vacation together), now is a good time to initiate serious discussions with your partner on how you'll negotiate these differences in the future.

Next, consider enrolling in a premarital counseling workshop, if you haven't already. (See the Resources section at the end of this book for more details.) Led by trained marital and family counselors, these classes aim to bring to

the forefront such big issues as finance management, dealing with in-laws, and childrearing philosophies—common
sources of marital angst that couples should discuss before
getting married (if only to ensure that each one knows
where the other stands, not necessarily to resolve disagreements). Many of these workshops are based on scientific
research on the types of relationship skills needed to survive
the often rocky road of marriage; they also strive to teach
couples successful forms of communication, such as learning how to express one's emotions, desires, and needs as well
as how to listen to your mate without insinuating that his
views and ways of doing things are Neanderthal. Many also
highlight factors that indicate whether you as an individual
are ready to tie the knot or not.

Learning how to talk about different points of view and
how to compromise on existing or potential conflicts are
other aims of these courses. Some religious affiliations offer
(and often require) these premarriage sessions, too. The
Unitarian minister who married Lawrence and me did her
own version of these sessions, and I found them excellent in
bringing added intimacy to the whole wedding planning
extravaganza. They enabled us to take time out from deciding what our cake should look like to talking about our
future and the challenges of married life, all of which rein-
forced how much I respected my husband. We also got
approval from our minister, which was a bonus to our relationship esteem. It's important to remember throughout all
the crazy planning that the event in question is ultimately
about your relationship and love, and the cake or the color
of your bridesmaids' dresses isn't all that important.

obsessive-compulsive

Every bride I spoke with experienced some bout of obsessive-compulsive disorder during the months leading up to the big event. Mine started with the Save the Date letters. Lawrence and I decided we would print them ourselves since they were, in fact, merely throwaway reminders. To my mind these little notes cheerfully announcing our wedding day and enticing our out-of-town guests to save that date for us set the entire tone of the wedding. Their importance grew to monumental proportions in my head. They represented something far more important, something along the lines of "This is the first impression everyone will have of our coming event, and it must be representative—not too flashy, but formal and fun. Nobody will get excited about our wedding if these letters aren't elegant and inspiring!"

In other words, I obsessed. There is a spectacular paper store in San Francisco that I hit one rainy Saturday morning not too long after we announced our engagement. I went alone. Lined up and down a twelve-foot-high wall of the store are hundreds of different types of paper, from Japanese rice paper with little specs of flower petals and leaves to imported Italian parchment. There was translucent kelly green paper with matching envelopes, decorative striped paper, the grocery-store brown-bag style, and San Francisco theme stationery. There was peacock blue, Chinese power-red, metallic shiny paper (that probably couldn't even pass through a laser printer), and glow-in-the-dark paper. There was confetti (to put in the envelope), ribbons (to punch through the top of a card for extra flair), and thousands of paint pens and calligraphy pens to address the equally challenging selection of envelopes on display.

I left the store empty-handed and rattled by the horrendous hour spent fingering each and every type of paper, imagining how it would look with "Save the Date" printed on top. (And let's not even get into the font and style of the card's wording, a process that took several rewrites and days of contemplation and discussion with my fiancé.) This experience only confirmed my fear that wedding planning would consume my mind and soul, and I'm not even the type of person who normally cares about such details!

Dara, who usually prides herself on not caring what others think of her, obsessed, too. She felt that all her decisions, from invitation to wedding dress style, were going to be judged, and she couldn't help worrying. As she was planning her debut into marriage, she started getting flashbacks to weddings she had attended in the past where guests snickered about the ugly bridesmaids' dresses or the weird lack of music/dancing/drinking. To calm her nerves she bought every wedding magazine ever published and even ordered all the back issues of *Martha Stewart Weddings* to give her ideas. She felt that if she missed one, it would be the one that contained the key ingredient to her perfect wedding.

Margo, 30, of Boston, Massachusetts, obsessed over the seating arrangement at her reception dinner. With 250 guests coming to her wedding, she didn't want people scrambling in a panic to get tables with their friends, so she spent hours assigning and reassigning people to their tables. She called and recalled her reception coordinator with endless changes. This is an example of the compulsive acts you may perform at some point during the wedding planning. My compulsion involved making lists of things to do. Every day I made a new list and took great satisfaction in scratching items off it but was agonized at the ones that never seemed to disappear.

Why this obsessive-compulsive behavior? One theory holds that, like it or not, our wedding day is a day of judgment in our society. Sure, our family and friends love us for who we are, but they will undoubtedly make mental notes on everything about the wedding, from the dress we wear to the flowers we choose to the music we play to the people we invite. Because there are so few occasions in which we get to formally present our sense of style, a wedding is often the first time in our adult life that we get to display it.

Besides, people gossip at weddings and typically view every aspect of the event as a reflection of the bride's (not the groom's) taste. We've all been to weddings in which guests made unfavorable comments on the reception menu (is there nothing vegan?), the bride's hair (*ringlets*???), the music ("Hello, you can't even dance to that!"), and the limited wine and beer bar.

As a bride-to-be you are putting on a production, and like all productions, whether in a theater or cathedral, yours is subject to criticism. Our culture is wired to critique what we see, and knowing that is partially what prompts this obsessiveness in many women who are engaged. Since it won't help you for me to tell you not to obsess (you'll do it anyway), I can only advise you not to obsess too much. Your wedding will be wonderful (trust me) regardless of whether you obsess over it or not. The choice is yours.

committed

On a more sentimental note, your engagement will be one of the most heartwarming emotional trips you'll ever take.

Not only will you and your mate feel sentimental about your pre-engagement history together the moment you decide to get hitched, but you may also feel a renewed passion (i.e., more sex!).

Despite the stress and all the preparations a wedding celebration demands, most brides-to-be will feel an overwhelming affection, indescribable joy, and an unyielding commitment toward their beloved. When Hope, 37, of New York, New York, got engaged, she had a transformation in the way she viewed her husband. She began looking at him differently, envisioning him as a father. She started looking at his face more seriously, wondering which features might come out in their future children. His sense of style suddenly didn't bother her as much. And when she saw older couples in their fifties and sixties, she took more of an interest in them, wondering how she and her husband-to-be might evolve as they grew old together.

There is a feeling of unrivaled acceptance that goes along with an engagement, which is a good thing to remember when the less savory emotions that go along with planning a wedding begin to wear you down. You may also find that once you're engaged, a door opens, and you will feel much freer talking to your fiancé about your future as a couple. Such topics as starting a family, buying a house together, deciding where you want to live for the rest of your lives, and even your personal views on childrearing may now flow freely in conversation, when just days before these topics were considered uncomfortable at best, but mostly taboo. There's nothing else like that committed feeling during the engagement, except perhaps the moment you share that commitment publicly in the form of wedding vows. So let's move on to the big day, shall we?

TWO

Something new

The wedding ritual is the first (and possibly only) celebration in which you and your future husband will publicly honor your commitment to each other, unless you plan to renew your vows at some point or throw fancy anniversary parties in hallmark years. Even if you're the type of gal to run off to city hall with your dashing partner one morning on a romantic whim, you'll still have to endure paperwork and be required by state law to recite your "I do's" in front of a judge and at least one witness. If you've managed to lead a relatively private engagement thus far, the wedding (or post-elopement announcement party) frequently reaps overwhelming attention from friends and folk who desperately wish to be part of this giant step you're taking.

Planning and participating in this highly ritualized ceremony (one of the few cross-cultural celebrations that exist in our diverse country these days) will shape your journey into wild, mysterious matrimony (assuming, of course, that this is your first time entering the jungle). Despite the trauma of wedding planning (see the previous chapter), preparing for this rite of passage will indubitably force your relationship to grow. You see, planning a wedding ceremony and reception is a microcosm of marriage.

As in wedlock, wedding planning requires that you and your husband-to-be confront the hard questions in life, many of which you'll be forced to address as a couple for the first time. For instance, how to handle parental involvement in your life (especially for those of you with overbearing parents or with folks who consider the wedding more *their* party than yours). Or how *not* to alienate your single friends during a time in which your main focus is to idealize the alternative lifestyle of marriage and all the domesticity that goes with that, not the joys of being sexy and single.

If you are planning a private ceremony (as opposed to one at city hall), you and your mate will naturally have to discuss the details of the ritual, including vows, readings, and music—all of which forces the two of you to contemplate and communicate what you find sacred in life and in love. The sacredness of it all may then lead to philosophical questioning of where spirituality or religion fits into your future—especially if children are a part of your marital plan (which is probably not your usual dinner conversation fodder). Spirituality is only part of the ceremony discussions; you'll also want to consider all the wedding traditions, determining which ones you find charming and which you find offensive. Through these discussions you'll get to witness how your individual upbringings have unknowingly influenced your current attitudes toward celebrations in general.

Wedding planning also forces you and your mate to make some fairly stressful financial decisions (especially difficult on the relationship if you're covering the wedding expenses yourselves). These will involve many talks (often heated) of priorities and put your communication and conflict resolution skills to the test. And perhaps for the first time you'll get to see how you and your partner handle the division-of-labor issue—when it comes to all the pre-wedding organization that must be dealt with. (Try not to get too discouraged on this front, ladies. It seems to be true, at least anecdotally, that grooms-in-waiting procrastinate on their tasks, which will drive you insane. And your mates may also tell you they don't have opinions on things when they really do, which you find out after the fact, but let's not dicker about details.)

If you're like most brides, you will have a stack of books on how to plan your wedding, so I won't bore you with my own opinions about pulling off this feat of endurance with poise and style. I'll leave that to Emily Post. But I will detail what I think every woman might want to consider as she prepares for the marriage rite of passage.

prenuptial rituals

If we go with the assumption that rituals are a human invention meant to ease anxiety associated with nerve-racking life events, emotions, or transitions, then some of the pre-wedding rituals make perfect sense in modern times. Call me a pop-anthropologist, but I must point out some of the similarities between bridal wedding rituals in this country, diverse as they may be, and the various coming-of-age rites of passage I've seen on National Geographic documentaries.

the bridal makeover

The bridal makeover consists of several sub-rituals. The most pervasive, perhaps, is the fasting ritual (or the less maniacal, though no healthier, pre-wedding experimentation of crash dieting). As I mentioned in the last chapter, dieting does nothing to ease a girl's anxiety. On the contrary, it tends to provoke hunger and a distinct edginess. In other rites of passage, fasting is used to invoke hallucinations, visions, or other forms of enlightenment. Sadly, dieting before the wedding rarely offers a bride insight into the world of marriage (except that it is truly a test of marital patience when your mate is sipping imported Belgium beer and popping cashew nuts as you sip water and steam your nonfat broccoli).

Still, the parallels are interesting, especially when you consider other sub-rituals of the bridal makeover, such as waxing, plucking, exfoliating, and frequenting the local tanning salon (though many of us would hate to admit it to our friends and dermatologists). After all, enduring pain and body mutilation is another common theme among rites-of-passage ceremonies around the globe. Then there is all the ornamentation that goes along with the makeover: the cosmetics, the exotic hairstyles, the manicures, the pedicures, the jewels, the veil (or other hairpieces such as crowns, flowers, and sparkly barrettes), the silky lingerie, the garter, the magical scent—all in an attempt to transform you into the mythical bride that our culture idolizes in bridal magazines and Hollywood remakes of *Father of the Bride*.

Not that I fundamentally oppose the bridal makeover. I admit it: I made a concerted effort to reinvent myself during the nine months between my engagement day and my wedding day. I endured daily forty-minute sweaty excursions on the treadmill at the company gym and hundreds of crunches (and I *deplore* abdominal exercises). I ate yogurt and an apple for lunch every day for a month straight, and I refrained from the post-workout binge of chips and chocolate. What's more, I signed up for a few sessions at the local tanning salon, which I justified despite my fears of skin cancer, because I wanted to get rid of the glow-in-the-dark bikini-strap mark that ran across my back and would be visible in my backless wedding gown.

The more anxious I became about wedding details, the more I became fixated on my appearance, including the status of my lingerie, which needed a major upgrade for the honeymoon. The realization that I was going to be photographed a zillion times to immortalize the day just added to the stress. Part of this makeover madness was simply a matter of my wanting to be decadent and feminine, since I rarely allow myself to indulge in girly things, such as getting my nails done or having my clogged pores (translation: zits) extracted by a professional (which, by the way, hurts if you're a novice like me). But I also know my hang-ups well enough to know that I tend to place far more of my self-esteem on my looks than I should. And it doesn't help that I'm a recovering perfectionist and wanted to look, well, the *p* word. Or that at age 30 I could no longer pass for the "youthful bride" look and had to aim for sultry sophistication instead.

Which brings me back to my original pop-anthropological point: The primping ritual perhaps comes from a girl's biologically driven desire to be sexually attractive to her mate. If you believe what some sociologists do—that marriage ultimately evolved so that a woman would have security in knowing her mate would protect and feed her while she occupies herself with the tremendous task of propagating the human race—it seems natural that the female compulsion to maximize her sex appeal is acted out during the marriage ceremony.

the bachelorette party

Going on with my quasi-anthropological analogy, let's take a look at the bachelorette party. According to my theory, these celebrations serve as a way to ease anxiety related to the momentous coming event. (At least that would explain the ubiquitous party accoutrement, alcohol, as well as a popular party gift: aroma-therapeutic relaxation bath crystals).

When executed in a way that matches the bride's style, these pre-wedding festivities really do help lower ritual-related stress, because the bachelorette party (and its virginal sister, the bridal shower) at its most fundamental level is about female bonding, a crucial ingredient to the well-being of all married and single women. Holding these girl-fests before the wedding reassures a bride that her female friends and family members—a girl's most vital support group—are by her side as she makes her way into the unknowns of marriage. They also help reassure all the brides' friends that even though another one of their single girlfriends is biting the dust, their friendships are still sacred.

These parties also serve a practical purpose: They help introduce all the various female team players in your life to one another. This is particularly helpful if your husband-to-be has female friends and family members whom your closest gal pals have never met or, for that matter, you barely know yourself. Sally, 26, of St. Louis, Missouri, whose maid of honor planned a traditional girly gathering with games, snacks, and, of course, alcohol (mind-altering substances that go along with my rite-of-passage theme), also pointed out that her pre-wedding parties offered an opportunity for her friends to learn more about the husband-to-be. For instance, one of the games they played involved Sally's having to guess the answers to various questions about her fiancé (name his favorite artist, for instance) that the maid of honor had secretly researched through a phone conversation with the man in question.

Because these parties are typically planned for you, they are one of the few rituals in the whole wedding process in which you can simply sit back, enjoy, and let your friends take care of all the details. And since you will probably put many of the guests on your wedding task force, it will offer an opportunity for all your friends to bond in a soulful way, unless, of course, someone does something funky like hire a male stripper. But let's not even go there.

These days, of course, the traditional bridal shower or bachelorette party has all types of hybrid variations, some of which involve both men and women. I'm all for cross-gender parties; they're excellent for introducing his friends to your friends and will make the wedding more fun because your guests will have met each other beforehand. But I do think there's a time and a place for a female gathering, if solely to carve out a space in which we can communicate with one another in our uniquely female way, a space that's especially critical for women to have upon entering marriage.

temporary moratorium on sex

Some couples abstain from nooky several weeks before the wedding in an attempt to stir up a little longing, spark some buried lust, and possibly even psych themselves into believing that they're still virgins. This is not recommended.

Sex is a stress reliever, and assuming you're not a virgin, keeping up your sex life while you prepare for your wedding will not only help keep you sane, but will also help keep you and your partner bonded throughout the stressful times. What's more, holding off on sex until the wedding night puts an awful lot of pressure on you to perform spectacularly then. You and your mate may be too exhausted from the wedding to pull off the best sex of your lives, too.

the attendants

If you believe the folksy explanation of why bridesmaids and groomsmen (or best women and best men, as my husband insisted on calling all of them) wear identical outfits and stand beside the bride and groom as they exchange vows, you know that their sole purpose is to confuse evil spirits, who presumably are trying to curse the bride and groom on their wedding day. With everyone dressed so similarly, how can the spirits tell who's who? Why the spirits are bent on marital doom is beyond me, but most folklore is rather gloomy, isn't it?

What particularly bothers me about this interpretation, though, is that it insinuates the primary role of our attendants is to serve as decoy and bear the brunt of the curse, which if you ask me is a tad selfish of the nuptial couple. Still, there's a ring of truth to their purposes even today when evil spirits have forsaken their invisible devil image and reveal themselves only in such dastardly forms as acne on the bride's chin or a splatter of pink lip gloss on her lily-white tulle. The primary role of our attendants is to keep us calm by their running around doing the various tasks we request or dealing with last-minute disasters. So in a way our attendants are still plucked from our group of supporters for their aptitude in dealing with wedding day phantoms.

Choosing the closest friends and relatives who get to be the few "best women" is tricky business, though. Naturally, you'll want to include your sisters and other close female relatives. If you're in your late twenties or thirties, you probably have been a bridesmaid once or twice before, fueling your obligation to include those married girlfriends in your own bridal party. If your husband has sisters, well, that just widens the pool of people you would love to include. And how can you exclude your best girlfriends—even if your familial bridesmaids already add up to four or five?

Since you can't include everyone (or else you'd barely have an audience), you may have to do some tactful explaining to some of your close friends. I suggest making it clear to those who may feel left out that your wedding party choices do not necessarily reflect those who are your favorite friends or most admirable supporters. They may, instead, reflect a family tradition or, as is often the case, a compromise due to the number of groomsmen your husband has chosen in cases where the bride and groom want a balanced number of attendants. You might also mention that your decision not to include them is absolutely no indication of how much you value their friendship. Then make it up to them by asking them to be part of the "wedding party" and inviting them to the rehearsal dinner or putting them in charge of one of the many tasks. Or ask them to do a reading at your ceremony.

Getting ready for the ceremony with your bridesmaids can be one of the best parts of the wedding. At least it was for me. The frenetic energy of getting dressed with the girls brought me back to our post-college Friday evening ritual of group primping for the night's revelries. There we were, almost ten years later, in the "bridal dressing room," plucking each other's eyebrows, fixing each other's bra straps so they wouldn't show in our gowns, sneaking peeks at the pre-ceremony cocktail party the wedding guests were enjoying downstairs, and sipping champagne. Make a concerted effort to revel in this time with your bridesmaids, because you might not get this type of connection with them until after your honeymoon. During the actual wedding and reception, you'll be so overwhelmed by well-wishers and the "wedding high" that you might not manage a single decent conversation with anyone.

the joining of clans

Once upon a time, weddings were meant to unite two non-blood-related families, first through the property exchange known as marriage and then through any resulting off-spring. Love (or even affection) between the couple in ques-tion was a secondary consideration to the respective par-ents' primary objective of bettering their economic position or power or social standing or whatever it was that prompted them to negotiate the union in the first place. True, some cultures still use this form of matchmaking, which I can only thank the local gods doesn't exist in this country. It's not that I don't value my parents' opinions on my choice of a lifelong mate, I just can't imagine being so integrally involved in their personal agendas.

These days, many of our families have not only very lit-tle to do with choosing our life partners, but their primary concern about our future family-in-law is whether or not the members of this new clan are kind to us. That doesn't mean family members—yours and your fiancé's—won't involve themselves in planning the event. Weddings are still largely a family affair. Virginia Morgan Scott, a licensed clinical social worker and marriage and family therapist in Santa Cruz, California, explains the clan connection as such: "Marriage ceremonies bond families and ritualize the opening of their doors to include a new member. Weddings, at their best, are a fun time to show off the family unity and culture."

You may even be surprised at how well your normally contentious family behaves during your celebratory occasion, making you wonder where your real parents disappeared to. In some cases a wedding can even make you closer to your family and in-laws. Linda, 32, of San Francisco, California, experienced this with her husband's clan. When wedding funds were getting really tight, prompting the worst fight the couple had ever had, Linda's fiancé called his dad to see if they could borrow $5,000, a request that was so stressful for him, he cried. After the honeymoon they paid back a part of the loan as soon as they could, but the dad sent back their check, saying that the money he gave was a gift and he didn't expect it back. This gesture was extremely moving for the newlyweds; it made them feel that the folks really believed in them as a couple.

Other times, though, weddings offer the opportunity to provoke familial tension. In fact, according to my interviews, parental tension is one of the biggest sources of contention in wedding planning. The tension could even indicate what lies ahead in your marriage. "Marital therapists sometimes ask a couple to tell the story of their wedding," says Scott. "The therapist then listens for indicators of the family dynamics, believing that the way the couple handled themselves during this first major family event is indicative of the strengths and weaknesses of their respective families." For example, did your fiancé's mother call your mate in private to complain about the wedding location, pitting him against your preferred choice? Or was the wedding overshadowed by tensions between your divorced parents, which were then shifted to you and your mate (as was the case with one woman I interviewed whose mother-in-law badgered her son because his father, her ex, got to invite more guests than she did)? Or were there deviant in-law issues (as was the case with another woman whose mother-in-law boycotted her son's wedding because she thought his fiancée wasn't good enough for him)? Or did your mother insist your fiancé don a tux for the occasion when he loathes such attire and would have preferred to wear a simple suit?

I've dedicated Chapter 7, Ghosts from the Past, to managing the in-laws and parents, a process that begins soon after your engagement when parental expectations, power struggles, and former parent-child roles often reemerge. Emotional life-altering events have a way of eliciting delinquent behavior among parents and their offspring. If you're in the throes of wedding planning and your mother-in-law is telling you that your hipster wedding dress isn't appropriate, while your mother is simultaneously planning an embarrassing New Age–type spiritual blessing for a toast, go ahead and skip to Chapter 7 for advice on managing the parental units before and after the big day.

"let's just elope!"

Any woman who has ever planned her own wedding has likely fantasized about eloping. Not only does eloping have a romantic sound to it, but it also makes your wedding low-stress, low-key, and low-cost. If you're the type of gal who loathes being in the spotlight, running off with your mate for a private ceremony may be the ticket. But I advise you to think it through carefully. I always dreaded the thought of being in the spotlight of a formal wedding, but once it finally happened, I loved sharing this special occasion with my family and closest friends. As a compromise, some couples go the route of having a private ceremony followed by a big party for family and friends. That way a girl can avoid the spotlight panic and having to model a dress on which everyone will have an opinion but still reap the benefits of hearing touching toasts, seeing loved ones get teary-eyed about your future, and getting wedding gifts.

When Marguerite, 32, of Indianapolis, Indiana, woke up one morning, her boyfriend of three months asked, "What do you think about getting married today?" Having had the you-know-when-you-know moment within days after meeting her man, Marguerite said yes in a blink. The two giddily booked it to city hall, filled out the requisite marriage license form, and then tied the knot later that day. That was more than two years ago, and Marguerite has no regrets. "None of the wedding traditions appealed to us," she says. "We're both shy. The idea of staging a wedding for friends and relatives gave me serious stage fright."

Elopement or not, very few weddings go unnoticed when it comes to family and friends. Marguerite's family, for instance, was very hurt that they were excluded from her decision to get married and the ceremony itself. What's more, they had never even met the guy. "My family forced a party on us when I brought my husband home to meet them," she says. "It was sweet, but we both dreaded it. I'm kind of the black sheep of the family, so it bothered me when people came up to tell me how great my husband was. I didn't want or need their approval." The moral of this story is, if you head down the elopement route, keep in mind that your family and friends will still want to participate in some form or fashion. You may get away with a low-key celebration, but you'll never get away with one that's scot-free.

all things sacred

Of all the tasks involved in wedding planning, fashioning a ceremony that reflects your unique values, personality, and spirituality is, hands down, the most important part of the entire wedding affair. So it was for me. The ceremony was the only aspect of the wedding that I persistently day-dreamed about during the months leading up to the event. I imagined the music, the setting, the lighting, the vows, and the readings over and over again, until I had the entire ceremony practically memorized long before the wedding rehearsal. Because my husband and I are not particularly religious, this presented an interesting challenge: How to create a ceremony that would invoke our spirituality in an authentic way and reflect our expectations and dreams for marriage?

religion: yes or no?

One of the first issues many couples grapple with when planning their wedding is whether or not to incorporate religion in the ceremony. If you and your mate are both religious and practice the same faith, this will of course be a non-issue for you. If, however, one of you is religious and the other is not, or if you practice different faiths, or if neither of you has stepped in a house of worship since you were forced to as a child, you will have to consider the religion factor. This is primarily because religious organizations are one of the main venues through which couples can legally marry (the other options being a judge, justice of the peace, court clerk, or anyone who has been legally approved to perform the ceremony in the state where you plan to marry).

What's more, for many families religious wedding ceremonies are the tradition and, in orthodox cases, the *only* venue in which a marriage is deemed legitimate. Keeping with tradition lets you be symbolically connected to your family's history and culture. Maya, 32, of Portland, Oregon, wanted to follow the traditional Jewish ceremony even though she and her husband, who is also Jewish, get in touch with their spirituality through nature rather than organized religion. For her, incorporating religion in the wedding ceremony was a way to connect with her cultural heritage and to bond with her grandmother.

If you and your future spouse are not religious, you may want to consider how bucking tradition will affect family members; they may feel hurt or disappointed in you if religion is boycotted in the ceremony or if you are marrying someone outside of the family faith. Joseph Kelley, Ph.D., adjunct professor of religious studies and theology at Merrimack College in North Andover, Massachusetts, explains why: "For some parents, having a child marry outside of the faith presents a clash between past ancestors and the progeny. As parents you're caught in the middle," he says. "There's also a sense of loss. When a child marries, the parents are, in a sense, losing their child. If the child is also moving away from the faith, that accentuates the loss. Parents may take that as a rejection."

In such cases, compromise and communication are the key to easing familial unrest. After all, your parents' insistence on a religious ceremony could be about their subconscious desire for all their current and future relatives to end up in the same afterworld, rather than their trying to control you. Mandy, 32, of San Francisco, California, was raised as a Catholic; her husband was reared as an orthodox Jew. Both sets of parents wanted their offspring to marry in their respective religions. Through many discussions Mandy and her mate found out that their families' primary concern was wanting the couple to realize what they'd both be giving up by marrying outside of their faiths. Once the couple made it clear to family members that their commitment to each other outweighed religious affiliations, they designed a ceremony that would reflect their multicultural commitment.

Mandy's clan wanted the couple to get married in the family church by a priest, but that would have meant that the groom's orthodox family wouldn't be able to attend, since they couldn't step foot inside a church. Coordinating a priest and rabbi for the ceremony turned out to be very hard, so they opted to get married by a family friend who was a judge and who would hold an interfaith ceremony in a space that everyone could attend. To include traditions from both religions in their ceremony, they opted for the traditional Catholic Unity candle, which was lit by members of both families. Then they had relatives read various poems and readings that had spiritual (though not necessarily religious) significance. In accordance with Jewish tradition, her husband stomped on a glass at the end of the ceremony.

vows and readings

Picking your readings is one of the most challenging parts of ceremony planning. For me it was a chance for my husband and me to reflect on what we as a couple deemed sacred and how we wished to support each other within marriage. It was important for us to embrace within these readings our reverence for nature, our passion for each other, and our desire to maintain our independence within marriage. Our readings—an Anne Morrow Lindbergh poem that stressed the importance of individuality in love, a passionate scripture from the Old Testament, and the Apache Wedding Prayer (which we've since discovered was one of the trendiest readings of turn-of-the-millennium weddings—so much for uniqueness) were a reflection of our souls and of the optimism we shared for our future.

Personalizing the readings and vows will also help you and your mate define what marriage means to you and what you want to experience through marriage. Helen, 33, of Washington, D.C., recalls one phrase from her vows that perfectly described what she and her husband wanted to do for each other: "increase each other's joy." Increasing each other's joy, she says, automatically requires that you treat each other with compassion and an open mind. And it encourages each of you to pursue your own life's passion and not forget who you are and what you want, even as you join as a couple. Helen and her husband still use the expression as a reminder of their promise to each other when one of them steps out of line.

symbolic acts

Sometimes symbolic acts—a kiss, a prayer, or (if you live in the Northwest) holding hands in a circle in a grove of trees—are equally effective, if not *more* effective, than spoken words for evoking the soul. Dr. Kelley explains why: "Words fail to express certain things. 'I love you' expressed in a ritualistic way [through a kiss or exchange of rings, for instance] is more powerful." Anne and Michelle, of San Francisco, California, who can't legally marry because California law doesn't recognize gay and lesbian marriages, designed a symbolic ceremony to express their lifelong commitment to each other. The morning of their marriage ritual, they privately planted a rosebush in their garden to symbolize that they were establishing roots as a couple and were making a commitment to care for it.

Then a few dozen of their closest friends gathered. Anne and Michelle drew a giant circle with chalk on the concrete patio in their backyard and asked friends to write and draw their wishes for them within the circle. For the ceremony they stood outside the circle and exchanged vows, telling stories of how they met and what they pledged to each other. Then, holding hands, they jumped into the circle. Michelle explains why: "In slave communities, couples would jump over broomsticks to symbolize their marriage. In other cultures, couples walk around a bonfire. We wanted a way to physically represent that we were moving from one state to another."

cherry-picking traditions

These days, with many of us waiting longer in life before tying the knot, more and more women are bypassing some of the traditional elements of wedding festivities. I believe that this is a function of being wiser and more confident in our individuality. Take the first dance. The concept may have been cute back in the 1940s when men and women were exceptionally savvy on the dance floor, fox-trotting and waltzing in sync. But these days the first dance is often a stressful element of the wedding festivities for those of us who struggle with the basic box step. Not only do you have to come up with a song that's neither cliché nor sappy *and* has rated-G significance for you and your partner, but you also have to take dancing lessons or fake the moves when the spotlight is on you. If you come from the half of our population who grew up with single mothers, then dancing with your father, who traditionally cuts in at some point, may feel contrived and uncomfortable. Neither my husband nor I wanted to be the center of attention while we danced, so we let the dance floor open on its own and then discreetly cued the band to begin Billie Holiday's "I Get a Kick out of You." We snuck in our first dance while no one was paying too much attention.

The bridal bouquet toss is another traditional component of weddings that some of us choose to bypass. Either we oppose the concept of singling out all the unwed women (not a cute tradition for many of your female guests who are over thirty and single and not too excited about either aspect), or we've hated being pulled into the bouquet mosh pit in weddings we've attended in the past. Or we don't want to throw our delicate posies into a den of flailing arms. (I once witnessed two women tackle each other and knock down an entire dinner table while trying to catch the bouquet.) Sure, the flower and garter toss can be a fun element to a wedding, but if they're not your style, there are alternatives.

Eva, 28, of Sun Valley, Idaho, was adamant about skipping this tradition (despite her mother's protest) and borrowed from a friend's alternative tradition instead: the marriage dance. During the reception she and her husband grabbed the mike from the DJ and called all the married couples onto the dance floor. The music started, and after a bit, they asked all the couples that had been married for one year or less to leave the floor. The music continued a little longer, and then they asked the couples who had been married for up to five years to step aside. Next, they asked the ten-year-anniversary couples to move over, and so on until there was only one couple left on the floor to dance the remainder of the song. That couple had been married fifty-five years, and Eva gave her bouquet to them.

Some traditions, of course, have religious or cultural associations, so the question of deleting or modifying them may not be easy, especially if you share your plans with your families, who might have other expectations for the festivities. Mandy and her husband, for instance, had a few heated discussions about whether or not to include chair dancing as well as other traditional Jewish circle dances at their reception. Her Jewish husband wanted them; she (reared Catholic) didn't, arguing that the majority of their guests were not Jewish and wouldn't know the dances. Their solution was to keep the reception secular (no traditional folk dancing) and give a nod to their respective religions at the ceremony. Amber, 30, of San Francisco, included her Middle Eastern heritage in the wedding celebration by throwing a Middle Eastern–style rehearsal dinner, complete with belly dancer. Since neither she nor her husband (a sixth-generation Caucasian American) is particularly religious, they stayed away from religious traditions altogether but did incorporate a unique mix of spiritual readings from a variety of cultures in their wedding ceremony, including one reading by Lebanese poet and philosopher Kahlil Gibran.

the wedding high

Many of the emotions mentioned in Chapter 1 will make cameo appearances on your wedding day. This may not be news you want to hear right now, but it's my duty in this book to be straight with you on what's to come. Besides, by the time your wedding day arrives, you'll be so used to feel-

ing emotionally funky that you'll handle the deluge of feelings just fine. Of course, you may fall into the group of
brides who zone out and enter an emotional void come W-
Day—the mind's way of dealing with feelings that are too
intense to handle. If you can help it, try to be as present as
possible. Focus on your breathing when your thoughts start
to drift. The high you'll get from all the emotions is too
good to miss out on. The following variations of beautiful
bride indicate how wedding day emotions may affect you.

the teary bride

The good news is that everyone loves a teary bride. The
image, in fact, is extremely endearing (provided that the
bride wears waterproof mascara). A bawling bride, however,
is not cute. In fact, a bawling bride may alarm her wedding
guests, who might secretly wonder if she's really happy
about her decision to get married. Of course, one can't control one's tear volume during such emotionally intense
times, so it's best to carry tissues with you so you can clev-
erly cover the look of anguish on your face—a look that's
primarily due to emotion overload.

My weepiness came and went throughout my engagement: when I was imagining the ceremony, when the harpist
we auditioned began plucking a Bach composition I used to
play on the piano when I was a girl (and, yes, I picked that
one to make my entrance at the wedding), and when other
recent brides shared their wedding stories with me. I was
pretty good throughout the rehearsal dinner toasts, which is
another teary time for many brides. Even when I locked
eyes with my husband-to-be as I was walking down the
stairs toward him at the start of our ceremony, I felt only joy
(though I'll admit I was shocked to look out at all the guests

and see some of *them* on the verge of emotional distress). But the moment our minister pronounced us husband and wife, all my emotions welled up within me. Our photographer (despite our request that no photos be taken during the ceremony) snapped a shot of my husband and me just as we turned around to face our guests. The emotion and joy on both our faces is so different from any other look I've seen of us, we thanked him for ignoring our instructions.

When on the verge of emotional overload, there are three things a bride can do: (1) Find a distraction. When Sally felt the tears coming during her ceremony, she made a point of looking at her husband's best man, whose calm smile soothed her enough to refocus on the ceremony instead of her near-tear outburst. (2) Remove yourself from the source. Of course, this only works outside the actual ceremony. Eva felt an emotional onslaught while she was gathering with the girls before the ceremony began. Her solution was to run into the nearest closet and lock the door. Taking a minor break gives a girl a chance to pull herself together and regain her composure. (3) Go with it! When at her wedding Linda's husband pulled out the wedding band she had fallen in love with but had decided was too expense because of all the other wedding costs, and so she'd use her engagement ring as a wedding ring, she burst into tears. She remembers *shouting* her vows, she was so full of emotion.

the stressed-out bride

You may be teary, but you also may be stressed. About five minutes before my wedding began, I started having a panic attack, afraid that when the processional music started none of the bridesmaids or I would hear our cue (we were going to descend stairs), leaving my husband-to-be and all our guests wondering if I had bailed! Agitated, I started sweating profusely beneath my silk and organza, and ordered the bridesmaids into the hallway. It must have been bad, because I remember the photographer pulling me aside and explaining that the wedding wasn't going to start until *I* gave the go-ahead. Who knew? At least getting clear on that minor bit of wedding protocol calmed me down for a few more pre-wedding bridal shots. (And, yes, I look distressed in those.)

You may be short-tempered with your bridesmaids or close family members, too. Most of them will hopefully chalk it up to stress, but in case you're worried about being a tad witchy on your wedding day, you might want to take this book to your bridal shower and read this part to your attendants so you can all laugh nervously about it. Eva can relate: "I had one moment of stress in which I snapped at my niece," she recalls. "All the bridesmaids and I had taken a van to the church from the lodge where we got ready, and there were three bags with us. My niece was carrying one that held a letter that my fiancé's grandmother had written before she died. With it was a handkerchief she had wanted her grandson's bride to carry down the aisle on their wedding day. My niece accidentally left the bag on the van. I felt bad about getting upset at her, but I was also pissed at myself for asking her to carry such an important thing." (In the end, Eva was able to contact the van service, and the driver came running to the church with the bag at the last minute, so there was a happy ending to this stressful tale after all.)

Getting the requisite bridal massage a day before your wedding may help lower the tension that has been building up over the past year or so. So will asking your attendants and family to deal with all the confirmation calls so you don't have to. That way, when the baker tells you she has no idea what you're talking about when you call the morning of your wedding to confirm the arrival time of your wedding cake, as happened to us when my husband called to check on it, you won't have to experience personally the panic and anger, which will just add to your stress. (By the way, we got our cake, but how that happened despite our "lost order" remains a miracle at Montclair Bakery.) Also, if you and your husband can work out a calming gesture ahead of time, that may help in the thick of stressful moments. Ann, 28, of Boulder, Colorado, said she and her husband devised a secret hand signal for stressful moments. As her father walked her down the aisle (and her face looked panic-stricken), her fiancé made his discreet "chill out" gesture, which instantly calmed her down—until her father stepped all over the train of her dress. Oh, well.

the blissful bride

Yes, each and every one of you will feel blissed-out at some point during your wedding. It may not hit you until after the grand entrance or the bombardment of well-wishers greeting you when you make your entrance at the reception, but hit you it will. And it will hit you hard—so hard that all the other stresses and emotions will fade into the background. All you will remember afterward is a blur of euphoria. For one moment in time you will be surrounded by so much love and optimism and happiness from all the people you care about most in life that you will be on a high.

back at the hotel...

The wedding high continues right on through your grand exit, replete with rose petals, birdseed, bubbles (or an arch of sparklers if, like me, you get married in a restored Victorian that won't allow your guests to toss organic materials onto their grounds but, oddly enough, will allow them to flail flaming sticks with flying sparks after drinking for five hours straight). The high will peak when you hop into your getaway car and your fans clap, catcall, and jump up and down as you drive away, honking and waving. You'll carry that high with you to that special place you've selected to bed down for your first night as husband and wife. Unless you fall into the ever-decreasing percentage of women who are still virgins on their wedding night and are nervous about having sex for the first time, the high will linger for as long as you can remain awake (which isn't very long for many new brides).

My husband and I spent our wedding night at the Mark Hopkins Hotel, one of San Francisco's grand old landmark mansions-turned-hotel, a place that holds many memories for us. When we first moved in together, we lived nearby and shared more than one moving conversation at the Top of the Mark, a bar perched on the top of the hotel that has outrageous vistas of the city and bay. I particularly love the lounge part because local legend has it that Judy Garland used to sing there way back when, and she's one of my girlhood idols. Our tiny suite overlooked the bay, the Golden Gate Bridge, the hills where we got engaged, our old neighborhood, and, if you crooked your neck a certain way, the street corner where we met four years before.

We opened up the chilled bottle of champagne, compliments of the concierge. (By the way, when you're making reservations for a hotel on your wedding night, by all means mention that you're getting married that day. Even if you aren't paying for the pricey "honeymoon package," the concierge may throw in a complimentary bottle of bubbly for the occasion. But just in case he or she doesn't, be sure to pack an extra one in your suitcase; you can never be over-burdened by champagne during moments like these.) There we sat—my husband in his dashing charcoal gray Italian suit with sexy shoes; me in my silk gown and organza wrap— beaming at each other and recounting the evening's events. At first we were a little stunned, so full were we of raw emo-tion and party stimulation. Then we became a little nostal-gic that the event we had planned, agonized over, and excitably anticipated for the previous nine months was sud-denly over.

Sally felt a similar nostalgia when she and her husband got back to their hotel following their wedding. They first sat in their suite and opened all the wedding cards they had received, mainly wanting to enjoy their lavish surroundings while they could. Sally didn't want to take her dress off. She knew she'd never be a bride again and wanted to linger in her gown as long as she could. When they were ready for bed, she recalls sitting on the hotel bed facing a mirror and watching her husband take her hair down, a process that involved removing close to one hundred bobby pins. Each little strand of hair tumbling down onto her face was a bit-tersweet reminder that her wedding day was over.

It didn't take long before Lawrence and I turned giddy. We talked about what each of us remembered during the ceremony and reception, and the guests, the food, the band, who was dancing, who was talking to whom and about what. You'll do this throughout your entire honeymoon, by the way, because images and conversations will hit you like flashbacks during the week after your wedding. Then I slipped into something a little more revealing, and I'll leave it at that—or my husband will kill me for sharing the details of our wedding night in such a public way.

Now a word on wedding night sex: You and your new husband will fall into one of two camps: those who collapse onto the bed in exhaustion and are asleep in two minutes or those who don't. While I don't have statistics on how many couples make love on their wedding night, I do know from my candid interviews that not all do, mainly because they are so tired. If you fall into the camp that doesn't, try not to put too much importance on wedding night sex. Sure, it's supposed to be a magical moment, and maybe it was back when it was trendy to get married as a virgin. But placing so much importance on one night of sex could lead to disappointment. Faith, 29, of Los Angeles, California, can't honestly remember if she and her husband made love on their wedding night, but she knows that if they did, it wasn't earth-shattering. As she put it, "You can't plan perfect sex, just like you can't plan the perfect orgasm. Two nights ago I had the best sex of my life with my husband in our kitchen, and it was completely spontaneous. Perfect moments happen only by accident or on TV."

honeymooning

You and your new husband are going to be in dire need of R&R and alone time after the wedding. Even if you take only a three-day trip to a low-key retreat a few hours' drive away from home, I highly recommend making the honeymoon a priority as part of your marriage celebration. Honeymoons are everything they are knocked up to be. Did I just write "knocked up"? Honestly, no pun intended. But now that my train of thought has turned sexual, let's just say that the honeymoon is the orgasm of a wedding celebration. It is a release of tension that in some cases has been building up for a year or longer. It is the climax of connection between you and your new husband. And it is the one aspect of the wedding celebration that is solely about you and your mate.

During your honeymoon you will relive the wedding several times over, recounting memories and reflections with your new spouse. You will get to hear your husband call you his wife for the first time, which will give you a fluttery feeling if you're the romantic type. You will receive countless numbers of congratulations and well-wishes from complete strangers you meet who find out you are on your honeymoon (people will come up to you and ask if you are on your honeymoon, because you will exude a glow the other weary-worn travelers do not have). You will also likely get more sex than you're accustomed to, simply because there are fewer stresses to dampen your libidos, and the newness of your surroundings will keep you and your partner in the mood—*especially if you go somewhere warm and relaxing*. (This is a point worth sharing with your fiancé as you debate the oft-contentious question of where to go.) You'll also have the novelty of spending more one-on-one time with your partner than you've ever had before.

Planning your honeymoon can be a little stressful, so it's important to get most of the agenda squared away before you leave. The point is to relax and enjoy each other, not figure out which train to take at midnight on the night you arrive. Even the free-spirited among us should take this bit of advice to heart. There are times and places for stressful traveling, but the honeymoon is not one of them, because most of you will still be unwinding from burdensome last-minute wedding organizing and the explosion of extroversion you will have just encountered. That doesn't mean that your great escape can't be adventurous. I'm just saying that it should be well thought out.

My husband and I went to New Zealand for three weeks, traveling all over both the north and south islands. One of our many adventures included a four-day backpacking trip, hiking twelve-mile stretches of mountainous terrain each day from one sleeping hut to the next. Despite the dastardly biting sand flies, the intermittent bursts of rain that left us soaking and chilled, the exhausting allergy attack I experienced for five hours each day, and meals consisting of Vegemite on crackers in the morning and half-cooked pasta at night, it was one of the highlights of our trip. The scenery, the solitude, and being thrust so deeply into nature with nary a soul around made this part of our honeymoon a near spiritual experience. After nine months of wedding planning, being so entrenched in nature with each other couldn't have been a more divine way to solidify our marriage. It wouldn't have felt this way, though, if we hadn't bookended our hiking adventure with prearranged stays at warm, dry guesthouses and hearty New Zealand meals consisting of racks of lamb and full-bodied cabernets.

Of course, even the most meticulously planned honeymoons have their surprises and, in some cases, disappointments. When Linda and her husband planned their honeymoon to Italy, they didn't expect that their prebooked private guesthouse, perched on a cliff overlooking the Mediterranean Sea, would come infested with scorpions. After one sleepless night staring at the spooks crawling on the wall, they headed to Florence, where Linda literally ran away from her husband in one of the main squares to call her mom and get the scoop on her opinion of the wedding.

Because you're going to be subject to the fumes of post-wedding exhaustion, don't be surprised if you and your husband get snappy with each other on your honeymoon. Certainly, it's not what you expect on a journey meant to celebrate passion, but it's the reality for many couples—especially those who go on honeymoons that involve extensive movement from one place to another. Did I mention it's a good idea to pick a destination that's *warm and relaxing?* I admit I lost my temper a couple of times on our honeymoon, generally when we were caught in one of the New Zealand summer rainstorms, hiking on a glacier with slick-soled sneakers, with my hair turned frizzy in the mist. Thankfully, my husband has an understanding nature and was able to chalk up my outbursts to PMS—I got my period about a week into our honeymoon, which was another bummer.

Despite the minor setbacks, I still get teary-eyed when I think of our honeymoon. It was the longest stint of time we'd ever spent together with nothing on our agenda except being with each other; we took each day in stride, and I wouldn't trade a single aspect of it for any other experience. Who knows when we'll ever get to take that much time off together again to tramp across undeveloped strands and forests? If you don't have the funds for a honeymoon, postpone the wedding until you do. Or put it on your credit card. Some things in life are worth the interest, and a honeymoon is one of them.

postpartum depression

The fun part about coming back from your honeymoon, rested and rejuvenated, is getting to relive your wedding again with people other than your husband. Not only are you likely to have pictures from friends waiting in your mailbox or email, but you will also have the photographer's pictures to anticipate. If you hired a videographer (is it just me, or is that one of the ugliest words in the English language?), the wedding video awaits your viewing, too.

Then there are wedding presents to be opened and the sign-in book to read. But one of the best parts of coming back home is getting to call all your girlfriends for details about the wedding *they* went to. You see, they will have a completely different take on the event, and they'll have stories and perspectives that may seem as though they went to an entirely different wedding. These conversations will fascinate you for days. They will contain vital information about the after-reception parties, including who hooked up with whom and other critical details you missed because you were surrounded the entire evening by guests telling you how beautiful you look—which isn't a bad way to spend the evening, I might add. They will also contain critical details about the expression on your husband's face when he saw you for the first time as you came down the aisle, as well as the way the sunlight cast an angelic halo around you and your husband during the ceremony.

After the welcome home excitement dies down, though, many women feel a little blue. The truth is that you'll never again have all your family and friends travel such long distances to meet in one place at one time to honor you and your husband. Weddings are special in that way. I felt hints of post-wedding depression as early as our honeymoon. New Zealand, such a lush and mysterious country, has more than its fair share of romantic vistas. I remember thinking a few times that a certain spot would be the perfect place for my husband to propose. Then I had to laugh as I remembered we had just gotten married! But the realization that that phase of our relationship was over made me a little nostalgic. So did the last time I tried on my wedding dress before sending it to the dry cleaners for preservation and boxing. As I stood before the mirror, I wondered if one day I'd have a daughter who would wear this very dress on her wedding day.

You also might feel a little lost on what to do with yourself now that you're no longer spending every spare moment of your free time planning a wedding. On the other hand, you may feel downright gleeful that you suddenly have your weekends, evenings, and lunch hours back. Try to ease back into your routine as slowly as you can. Trust me, there are plenty of tasks that await you as a newlywed. We'll go over these in the next chapter. They will consume your life if you let them (especially the name-changing part if you decide to take on a new name). So take a few weeks off after you get home and make a concerted effort to transfer that relaxed attitude you acquired during your honeymoon into the real world that you and your mate are about to enter as husband and wife.

THREE

*M*arriage: the business

All of you romantics out there are going to loathe the very notion of this chapter, so go ahead and slap me (or my book) now, then get over it and read on. Like it or not, marriage is a business of sorts. Owning up to your role in the enterprise of matrimony, a merger between you and your husband's individual ambitions and goals, will help you through the transition in which you will become a partner instead of the CEO of your future. This is *not* an easy transition, I might add, especially for those of us who lived alone before marriage and are accustomed to making decisions free from consultation (or confrontation, as is often the case) with our significant other. As in business, the marital merger is also not easy if one of you is power-hungry, uncompromising, or a control freak—personal attributes that lead to neither good business nor good love.

Tying the knot is the equivalent of taking your relationship public, asking your most ardent supporters to approve your choice of a life partner and to continue their support of the pending merger through good times and bad. The vows you exchange during the wedding ceremony are, in fact, your mission statement on marriage, your personal code of ethics, which is why it's important to evaluate and modify these vows (or write your own) according to your joint philosophies on matrimony.

Once you return from your honeymoon, which you will have gone on immediately after the wedding if you took my advice in Chapter 2, you will be thrust into the task of reorganizing your life, making your day-to-day more conducive to your and your partner's daily rhythms and long-term goals. Even if you're one of the 50-plus percent of couples who live together before getting hitched, the emotional intensity you experience when you and your partner go public will require some measured adjustments to your lifestyle.

the paperwork

Not only is marriage a business, but marriage is serious business. With wedlock come certain state-determined rights and privileges, which is one argument for same-sex couples having the legal right to marry (and the fact that they don't is a blatant affront to their civil liberties).

Upon tying the knot, couples earn the right to file joint income taxes, participate in each other's health insurance plans, and receive each other's Social Security, or disability, benefits. A married couple can get family rates for insurance, gain admittance to hospital intensive care units if, God forbid, one partner ends up there, and make some medical and financial decisions for an incapacitated spouse. Other legal perks involve the right to become a citizen of the United States (if one partner is alien and citizenship is desired) and, in the event of death, to automatically receive a share of the deceased partner's estate (unless deemed otherwise in a will or prenuptial agreement).

To effect these rights, one must first prove that one is married, and that starts by getting a marriage certificate. So your first order of business will be to obtain one. A marriage certificate is different from a marriage license, which you and your husband applied for before the wedding and signed at the ceremony along with your officiator and a witness or two. A license is a state document that allows you to get married, while a certificate is proof that you are. The marriage certificate is not automatically sent to you after tying the knot; you will have to request an authorized copy of it from the county clerk's office or the county recorder or registrar's office, depending on the state you live in. Usually there is a fee that goes along with this request. And there's a time delay, so don't get too excited about receiving this document as soon as you return from your honeymoon.

The next order of business involves your employer, who brokers your relationship with the IRS. Since payroll deducts income tax from your paycheck and since Uncle Sam cares deeply about such things as your marital status (despite the fact that he never gives wedding gifts), both you and your spouse will need to fill out new W-4 forms indicating your recent status change. You may want to readjust your withholdings while you're at it, so go ahead and skip to Chapter 6, Money, to find out why before tackling the paperwork. Note: If you're planning to change your name or address, too, wait until you're ready to announce the New You before attempting these updates as well as the ones mentioned below. Otherwise, you'll have to deal with the same paperwork twice.

The next stop is updating your safety nets, which include retirement savings, life insurance, and health care policies. If you and your spouse have 401(k)s or similar retirement savings plans with your employers, you may want to change the beneficiary on your accounts to reflect each other. You may also want to consider maxxing out your contributions (if you haven't already) to help lower your combined income tax. You'll read about this in the Money chapter, too.

If you have life insurance policies through group plans with your respective companies, change the beneficiary to reflect your partner as well. And, finally, you may want to reconsider your health care coverage. Compare your policy with that of your spouse and decide if it makes sense to keep separate plans (because both are good and cheap, for instance) or to put both of your names on one policy (which may make sense if one coverage is much better than the other).

The next line of business for all you traditionalists out there is initiating the onerous task of changing your name. The question of whether or not to change your last name deserves discussion since many of us grapple with the choice. We'll get to that debate in the next chapter. For now, let's focus on the logistics. Effecting a name change varies from state to state, but in most cases you will typically need one document to get started: your marriage certificate. Once you have that official document in your possession, make twenty copies of it and then tackle the following governmental and private organizations that care about such things as your identity, in the following order:

1. SOCIAL SECURITY ADMINISTRATION. Getting a new Social Security card is the first step because other organizations require proof that you've already effected the change through the SSA. Do not under any circumstances attempt to get a new Social Security card in person. You will have to wait in a tireless, depressing, bureaucratic line for several hours, and you still won't walk away with a new card. Instead, go online (www.ssa.gov) or call (800-772-1213) to get the official name change form sent to you by mail. Then fill it out and mail it back along with your *original* marriage certificate and a self-addressed, stamped envelope. If you've filled out this form correctly (don't ask me for tips on that; I'm severely inept at form-filling, and it took me two attempts to get it right), you'll receive a new Social Security card within a couple of weeks. And the SSA will return your marriage certificate. (It might be slightly crumpled and have coffee stains on it, so don't plan on framing it.)

2. **DEPARTMENT OF MOTOR VEHICLES.** Once you have your new Social Security card, it's time to hit the DMV. To be perfectly frank, in my interviews for this book I found quite a discrepancy when it came to which to tackle first, the DMV or the SSA. Some women were able to get a new driver's license before getting a new Social Security card, but others (myself included) had trouble executing this in that order, resulting in multiple trips to both places. To be safe, make the DMV your second stop and call ahead to find out exactly what you'll need to bring: your new Social Security card, the original copy of your marriage certificate, current driver's license (which they'll confiscate), and your car's pink slip—so you can update your vehicle's registration while you're at it. If you have moved recently and wish to change your address, too, go ahead, but be sure to bring a copy of a recent bank statement or utility or other bill indicating your new address just in case they need proof.

At the DMV you will fill out a form requesting the name change. Then you'll get to pose for a new driver's license photo, which will give you an opportunity to right past photogenic wrongs. You'll also get to sign the license with your new signature—an aspect of the whole process that took me by such surprise, I signed my maiden name instead. This minor mishap has caused me some problems at the bank, so

take my advice and practice your new signature ahead of
time (to prevent being put on the spot and then finding yourself beholden to a signature style that irks you). Ask the
DMV processor to update your vehicle registration and
voter registration information while he or she is updating
your files. (The DMV may do this anyway, but it never hurts
to be ultra anal when it comes to paperwork.)

Here are a few more car-related details now that we're on
the topic: If you're paying a bank loan on a new car, the bank
is actually holding your pink slip (which is why you couldn't
find it in your files). You'll therefore need to initiate the
name change on your vehicle registration with the bank, possibly by sending them another name change form and/or a
copy of your marriage certificate. They will then give the
updated vehicle registration information to the DMV.
Meanwhile, the bank will update its records for your loan.
Finally, you'll need to inform your car insurance company
about your new name (possibly by sending them another
copy of your marriage certificate). You will then be done
with car-related updates, but keep in mind that several weeks
will probably pass before you get to tuck that new driver's
license into your wallet, so be patient.

3. FINANCIAL INSTITUTIONS. What a headache! Let's start with your
bank account. After marriage you and your mate may want to
revamp your entire financial bookkeeping system, so you
may want to discuss the overall financial plan ahead of time
and kill two birds with one stone (changing the name on
your personal account and opening up joint checking and
savings accounts, for instance). We'll discuss all financial
matters in the Money chapter later on. To effect the name
change you'll once again need to show the bank a copy of

your marriage certificate, so go ahead and tuck that into your bag before you go.

Next in line: credit cards. These vary in terms of formality. Some companies will let you tell them your new name over the phone; others require you to mail in a copy of your marriage certificate. If you have IRAs, other retirement funds, trust funds, or any other kind of financial property held privately or coordinated through work, such as flexible spending accounts and direct deposit arrangements, you'll also want to inform the administrators of these accounts of your new name.

4. **OTHER VARIOUS ORGANIZATIONS.** What follows is a list of other important documents you won't want to forget as you endure the name change marathon: passport, utility bills (including your Internet provider, which is easy to forget if you're billed automatically through your credit card), student loans, other loans, apartment lease or mortgage/home title documents, gym membership, airline mileage clubs (perk: if you and your husband share the same last name, it's much easier to share miles), club memberships, newspaper and magazine subscriptions, and alumni organizations (include your maiden name as a middle name so former colleagues can find you, otherwise you risk breaking down that professional network you've been working on since college).

the business plan

Typically, the business plan is discussed long before marriage—even before the engagement. Rarely is it discussed in business terms; usually it's in terms of pleasure, such as what your dreams and goals are for the future. Honestly, discussing the general plan—at least in the short term—is one of the most inspiring and romantic aspects of being a newly-wed. It's a chance to focus on your joint optimism for good things to come.

One couple I interviewed went so far as to design a five-year plan after tying the knot. They laid out their ambitions and dreams: working for two years, then each going back to school, and then having a baby. Naturally, the plan changed over the course of three years after their marriage ceremony, partially due to the fact that one of them lost a job. Most of the women I spoke with in interviewing for this book agreed that the plan always changes—it may be an unexpected pregnancy or a parent falls ill and moves into your home six months after you get back from your honey-moon. So, naturally, the agenda is designed to evolve and accommodate the unexpected. The goal, really, is to have your future expectations and dreams expressed so that you and your partner have something to strive for.

While I'm hardly suggesting that you and your mate schedule a meeting to discuss your marital business model (I'm not *that* hardcore!), I am suggesting that you make a point to engage frequently in discussions about your future, covering the following: personal goals (educational aspirations, travel desires, and how much time you would ideally like to spend with each other and with friends), professional goals (which could include such prospects as a job relocation or career change), family goals (how much time you want to spend with the folks and when you want to start your own family), and financial goals (which could include saving for a house, paying off debt, starting up a business, and how and when you'd like to retire).

Warning: You and your partner probably won't have the same short- and long-term goals. You may, in fact, have conflicting aspirations. What's more, one of you may be a plan-making stickler while the other finds the very notion of drawing up a personal timeline to be inhibiting and anal, wishing instead to take each day in stride. Discussing your future plans often initiates fighting, especially if you disagree on the general direction of where your marriage should go.

None of these scenarios is cause for worry. Like all things in marriage, you will need to work as a team, respecting each other's visions while constantly expressing your own individual needs. We'll talk more about how to negotiate differences in just a bit, so don't get your underwear in a curl, as my husband is fond of saying whenever I get uptight.

setting up shop

Statistically, about half of you reading this will have lived with your mate before tying the knot. For you, getting your house in order after the wedding will be less of a task than it will be for the other half who are orchestrating a move on top of dealing with marriage paperwork. Still, both groups will go through a period of adjustment after the wedding, so don't breeze over the rest of this chapter if you think you already know everything there is about living with your lover. Frankly, it's an ongoing lesson.

If you're new to cohabitation, you and your husband have the novel opportunity to look for a new place together. I highly recommend moving to a new home or apartment within the first year of marriage unless your post-wedding funds just can't foot the bill or if one of you has a killer pad and is willing to start anew in terms of furniture arrangement and décor. If you were living together before marriage, you may be wise to look for a new place as well. This I recommend because living in new surroundings will reinforce your new beginning and naturally encourage the two of you to create a Luv Shack that will accommodate all your new wedding gifts and those expanding nesting desires that many of you will experience during the first year.

If you aren't able to begin your marriage at a new abode, at least consider giving the old homestead a makeover. Even if all you do is paint the walls and rearrange the his and hers furniture so that neither one's personal items dominate the overall vision, the change will help solidify your new partnership. Setting up shop is a bonding experience, one that in the end will produce a home that reflects both of your unique styles and spirits (if you're the romantic type who believes the home is a reflection of the soul). That doesn't mean the bonding experience is always an easy one, though.

Those of us who were faced with the blank canvas of an apartment or home within the first year of marriage can attest to the amount of heat that often arises between lovers over such mundane decorating decisions as paint color, light fixtures, window coverings (the curtains-versus-blinds debate), and furniture. If you marry an architectural engineer like I did, these discussions will carry even graver consequences, such as whether or not to knock out an entire wall that will demolish your sacred writer's cove. I call these the decorating wars. If you and your mate have huge clashes of opinions on what to do with your living quarters, such debates over home décor can become so passionate that you may feel that you are fighting for your very life. You are not, of course, but in many cases you *are* fighting over what seems like part of your identity.

The truth is, unless one of you really doesn't give a

twig about it, when you and your husband begin decorating and organizing your home, you will be forced to practice one of the greatest skills in marriage: compromise. If your husband insists on keeping his Heineken shot glass in the antique china cabinet along with your great-grandmother's crystal champagne glasses from the 1920s, so be it. That shot glass is important to him, and you need to get over your *Architectural Digest*–induced display case perfectionism. Likewise, when your husband begs you to remove all your girly bath gels and soap from the bathtub rim because it makes the bathroom look cluttered and feminine, he will simply have to deal, because your bath gels are sacred.

When you have your heart set on the swank blue velvet sofa and he's begging for the olive bunker-type couch built for comfort, you're going to have to put your dream purchases aside and look for a sofa you can both live with. The bottom line is that in marriage you sometimes don't get what you *really* want for your home—the feather-soft mattress, the Provence-style china—but neither does your husband. What's important is that you respect each other's tastes and work on compromises. For a marriage to work it's critical that both partners feel at home when they are at home.

Which brings me to a few thoughts on what makes home sweet home for a sexy, rich marriage:

1. **AMPLE CLOSET SPACE.** I can't tell you how often the topic of closet space entered the discussion when I was interviewing women for this book. Here's why I believe closet space ranks high in terms of supporting a sexy marriage. When our silk sweater sets and linen skirts are being smashed against the closet wall due to our husband's frayed leisure wear, the key component to our external image becomes compromised

and wrinkled. In addition, closets serve to hide junk that we don't wish to see. If we lack proper storage space, our clutter will be exposed, and we will also begin to feel that our privacy is under attack. Because closet space is such an issue, there are a few things you can do. For starters, redo your closets, making them bigger if possible, and add shelves to create more space. Candace, 33, of New York, New York, and her husband use canvas boxes to store clothing used in seasons other than the one they are currently in, alternating pants, skirts, shirts and sweaters when the weather changes. Amber, 30, of San Francisco, California, who is a minimalist, and her husband, who is not, live in a one-room loft, which requires them to devise creative storage options as well. They took stock of the things they used daily, weekly, monthly, and yearly, and then put into storage all the items they wouldn't touch for another six months or so. Tip: Armoires and trunks make chic storage options.

2. **THE MARRIAGE BEDROOM.** Just think about all the profound events that often transpire in the bedroom: making love, snuggling under the covers to discuss the day's happenings, dreaming, sleeping in late, recuperating when ill, and even conceiving a baby. Because some of the most life-affirming and life-altering events occur in the bedroom, it's critical that you focus your decorating skill on this sacred chamber. Let's start with the bed. Make it a priority to find a mattress on which neither of you wakes up in the morning with an aching lower back or limbs that have fallen asleep due to lack of circulation. After all, a bed that is cozy gives you and your partner all the more reason to connect in the only way an intimate couple can. Mattress buying is not an easy task, though, considering that some like it hard and others like it soft. I've found that, in general, the more money you're willing to

spend, the better your chance of finding one in which you'll both sleep like babies. Go to mattress stores in person and spend a good hour lounging on top of the various models and speaking with reps about your preferred sleeping positions. Then purchase the type that includes a comfort guarantee, so you can return it for a full refund if you don't find it suitable after all. While you're at it, hit the bedding sections of your favorite department stores and take extra care in purchasing two expensive pillows (don't even think about the $9.99 specials). I've found that the more money you're willing to spend on pillows, the less likely it is that they will transform into clumpy balls of cotton over the years. Since pillows are typically nonreturnable, spend ample time mocking sleep on the display models and asking the salespeople lots of questions about the right style for your particular sleeping positions. You may have to go through several pillows before you find the right match, but at least you'll have extra ones in the house for overnight guests. As for the rest of the bedroom, my advice is to keep it simple and pure, devoted strictly to relaxation. In other words, move the home office out of this sacred realm and into a corner of the living or dining room instead. Think B & B retreat while planning the room. Doing so will help support a sexy love life. After all, how aroused can you be if, while making love, you're staring at your blinking computer screen that is reminding you of unfinished business?

3. SPACE FOR ENTERTAINING. Many couples slip into nesting mode soon after their wedding, due partially to the surplus of domestic goods (china, flatware, cooking tools) received as wedding presents. If this sounds familiar, I suggest that you focus your decorating endeavors on an area devoted to entertaining guests, because your social life will soon make room for more home-based gatherings. Since the entertaining den is typically going to be your living room, consider the following items key for good times: a comfortable sofa, several chairs of various sizes and shapes, a coffee table large enough to accommodate several glasses and plates of food, and a diverse mix of CDs.

4. A ROOM OF ONE'S OWN. Perhaps the most important element when setting up shop is carving out a space that's devoted entirely to one's self. It's imperative that both you and your husband do this. These areas should be separate from the bedroom and, if not separated by a wall and door, at least visually defined by a shoji or other screen or curtain or, at a bare minimum, an area rug. Creating this space will help maintain a sense of self and a separate identity from that of your husband, giving you and your partner the restorative solitude you need to maintain a vibrant relationship. My personal space has always been my office since I work at home. Having a small room—a walk-in closet in one apartment where we lived, an enclosed porch in another—with a door that I can close is imperative for separating my professional from my personal life. Otherwise, I'm apt to procrastinate at work and spend my days wandering into the bedroom for a nap or the kitchen to attack the refrigerator. In my office I hang the art and pictures that have special meaning for me, and I keep a shelf filled with my professional books and personal CDs. My husband's space is in the spare bedroom, where he keeps his desk and photography equipment. He also dominates the shed in back with his multiple sets of tools and home improvement paraphernalia. Other women I interviewed carved out their own space in creative ways. Paula, 31, of Spokane, Washington, has a rocking chair in a well-lit corner of the house where she retreats when she needs some space. Her husband tinkers in the basement when he needs time alone. Barbara, 30, of Staten Island, New York, finds respite on her deck where she cultivates a garden, which she says "keeps her sane." And Kathleen, 27, of Portland, Oregon, who is the mother of a toddler, has set up a table in the corner of the living room where she can retreat when she has the time and mental energy to draw (which isn't often, she admits).

5. R-E-S-P-E-C-T. The last element that will assist your efforts at setting up shop is a hearty dose of respect for the way your partner operates on a day-to-day basis. If he's the type who leaves a paper trail wherever he goes—scattering letters on the coffee table, bills in the kitchen, important documents across the desk in the dining room—it's very important to come up with a compromise for dealing with clutter, such as gathering all the paper into one stack that will live indefinitely on a designated table in the foyer, or creating one or two junk drawers into which you can chuck anything you don't feel like dealing with. Mindy, 25, of Somerset, New Jersey, and her husband agreed that their kitchen table would always be a wreck, marking it as the spot where they could dump their stuff unabashedly when they came home from a hectic day. Coming up with a joint plan for where household items should go will help each of you feel as if you're playing an active role in setting up shop. Plus, doing this task jointly will prevent your husband from constantly asking you where things are.

time management

Those of you who are novices at cohabitation will soon discover that in forming the marital merger, the adjustments you need to make aren't limited to sharing space. You'll also be adapting to each other's schedules and biorhythms (who knew he really goes to bed at 9:30 every night?). In speaking with dozens of other married women on the matter, I've found that there are two main areas of time management that require fine-tuning upon getting hitched.

The first, believe it or not, is finding time to spend with your mate. Single friends may scoff at this dilemma, believing that if you live with your partner, you spend all your time at home frolicking nude around the kitchen with a twig of rosemary behind each ear, but that's generally due to their lack of experience in the matter. Certainly, you see your partner every day, but in most respects you see the roommate version, not the passionate lover or the future-father-of-your-children version.

When you take both of your work schedules (throwing in the possibility that one of you is a workaholic or has discouraging work hours, such as leaving the house at 5:30 A.M. or getting home after 10:00 at night), and add your plans for working out several times a week, spending time with friends, spacing out in front of a window listening to CDs, going to Bikram yoga, and taking an acting class, you're dramatically reducing the amount of time available for bonding with your mate. But wait, there's more.

As a married gal you will now be dividing any remaining free time designated for your husband between two people: your lover and your roommate. With your roommate (who is really your lover disguised in sweatpants and athletic socks) you will be divvying up daily household chores—making dinner, doing the dishes, cleaning, folding laundry, paying bills, and returning phone calls. And this, my friend, is hardly considered quality time. That leaves only a very few hours (or minutes, on some harried days) available to actually spend with your husband going over the day's events and exchanging sweet nothings. In fact, the stress of all your new roles shared as a married couple means you'll need even more time than ever to reconnect.

While I don't mean to de-romanticize marriage, I do mean to provide you (especially those of you who have never lived with your mates) with a reality check so you don't think there's something wrong with your marriage just because you and your man are discussing the virtues of MCI versus AT&T instead of sipping a velvety cabernet and making mad, passionate love in the Jacuzzi. Before you tied the knot, many of you may have shared only one role with your partner, that of lover. As a married woman you'll be sharing all sorts of roles with your husband: financial consultant, career adviser, social coordinator, in-law mediator, family therapist, nurse, cook, cleaner, travel coordinator, and, oh yeah, lover.

The lack of time together is even harder for many couples when one partner needs more one-on-one time than the other. Jill, 25, of Kansas City, Missouri, experienced this dynamic soon after tying the knot when she suddenly found herself without a job (this was during the dot-com massacre of 2001). To make ends meet until Jill found work again, her husband took on a second job, which severely limited the amount of time they got to spend together. Lacking interaction with others during the day, Jill started calling her husband at work—sometimes seven or eight times a day. Out of sheer embarrassment she'd try to disguise her voice so the secretary wouldn't know she was calling so much (but the secretary always knew, responding, "Oh, hi, Jill"). Eventually they were able to work out a compromise: Jill began spending more time at home with her family, so her needs for companionship weren't entirely focused on her husband. When she got a new job, their relationship fell back into pre-layoff harmony.

While every couple has unique time restraints and needs, I believe it's vital for a healthy marriage to spend quality time together *every* day (or at least as close to every day as possible). There are many ways to sneak this in; the only requirement is that you preserve this time for connecting, not discussing roommate-type issues. Many couples find that the only time they have to connect is during dinner, which they try to always eat together. Some even attempt to capitalize on the opportunity, turning the dinner hour into a romantic event. That's how Sharon, 28, of Oakland, California, and her husband connect. They cook dinner together every night, complete with candlelight and music. Candace and her husband claim 10 P.M. and beyond as their private time. If the phone rings, they don't answer it. This time is preserved for reconnecting. She says it's what they need to do to ensure that their marriage will work. Sophie, 27, of Dallas, Texas, and her husband make an effort to involve each other in their personal lives. They occasionally participate in each other's favorite form of stress relief. That means her husband joins her at her yoga class, and she watches him play soccer.

Another route that many couples take to ensure the daily bond is going to bed at the same time. (This is obviously not a good option for night owls who marry morning birds.) If bedtimes aren't in sync because one of you hits the sack early, you can at least designate a particular time to cuddle each night. Then when one of you dozes off, the other can slip out of the room and resume his or her late-night amusements.

In addition to spending a little time together daily, it's very important for couples to preserve a weekly "date" for themselves. Whether that date is for dinner or for a daylong hike on Sunday, sticking to the routine will ensure that you get a chance to bond in a fun way, as opposed to a roommate way. This is essential for keeping a healthy, sexy marriage. Honor this plan especially when you and your husband are busiest.

Deborah, 30, of Santa Cruz, California, and her mate commute in opposite directions. That combined with her soccer practice and weekly night out with a girlfriend leaves little time for bonding with her partner. When their schedules begin to get really hectic, they bring out their calendar and block out the first free weekend as a time in which neither of them is allowed to make plans. They spend that weekend together, doing something spontaneous.

The second area in time management that requires adjustment for those moving in with their partner for the first time is learning to spend time with your husband *without* interacting. This will be a change because in the past when you've gotten together, the general plan was to interact. What's more, both of you were likely on your best behavior, not spacing out in front of the TV or eating an entire bag of chips for dinner, as you might have when living alone. Living with your lover, on the other hand, requires that you allow each other adequate downtime. It's the only way to restore energy, especially for those of us who are introverts.

This downtime is especially critical during the witching hour—that span of time after work during which you and your husband are transitioning from public to private life. This is often a stressful period, especially if things went wrong at the office or you're still stressed about a nasty coworker or you're mentally preoccupied with a deadline you didn't meet. Allison, 27, of Dallas, Texas, found the witching hour the hardest part of adjusting to marriage. When she was first married, she worked two minutes away from the house and was still wound up from the day when she arrived home. Her husband, who had a different schedule, came home with his own moods, too, due to the day's events. "It was a learning process, since we hadn't lived together before marriage," she says. "We learned that it was smart not to talk to each other for about an hour after we got home from work."

Other ways of dealing with the witching hour include working out immediately after work or meeting friends for a post-work power walk or cocktail. Barbara and her husband try to go on walks together when they get home from work; this helps them unwind and sets them up for better connecting later on. When they get back from their walk, they each do their own thing for an hour or two and then prepare dinner together.

division of labor

Back in the olden days, the marriage contract went something like this: Man must provide food, clothing, and shelter for wife and children; woman must manage domestic responsibilities—cooking, cleaning, childrearing, and other household duties. A woman was not entitled to keep any money she earned (such income was considered the sole property of her husband), nor could she legally own land or property. If man found woman's services and/or allegiance to him unsatisfactory, he could physically reprimand her.

Put more bluntly, domestic violence was once a husband's legal right. You know that phrase "rule of thumb"? It comes from a court decision in which a judge determined that a husband could beat his wife with a stick no thicker than a human thumb.

Makes you sick, doesn't it? But my point isn't to discuss the chilling inhumanity of the former rights of women in our country. Still, it's interesting to note how drastically our rights have changed over the past century. Once upon a time our legal institutions instructed families on how to divide the labor in a household. Now those decisions are left up to the couple, and they are often what spurs the most debate (and headache) when it comes to dealing with love and marriage.

For this book I asked dozens of married women what they felt the role of a wife was. Many snorted in response. Others guffawed. The general consensus was that the word "wife" was a turnoff, obsolete, outdated. It had too many negative connotations from times past when women were not valued outside of the home (or inside, either, in many cases). My interviewees associated the word "wife" with a woman wearing an enormous smile, pointy bra, and frilly apron, standing at the stove, always sacrificing her own needs for those of her family.

The terms "team player" and "partner" are how many of these women refer to themselves rather than "wife" (although some simultaneously admitted that they love hearing their husband use the word in introductions). The truth is, the role of a wife these days is amorphous, since she typically shares the same duties and responsibilities as her husband, at least in terms of bringing in money and doing chores around the house. Though I can't speak from experience, I've heard from others that the real specialization of roles begins when you and your mate decide to have a baby. Then the spousal duties tend to become more defined, with many women taking on the domestic responsibilities (at least while they're still breastfeeding) and men financing the whole shebang through their jobs. Of course, this, too, is changing with more and more women returning to work after a brief maternity leave and more and more men choosing part-time schedules, working at home, or taking time off completely after the arrival of their offspring in order to assist in childrearing.

Before kids, though, the division of labor is relatively straightforward, though rarely established without heated arguments, I've found. Husband and wife determine what each will contribute to the household, whether it is to provide income, manage the finances, do the dreaded laundry, or contribute in part to all of the above. Most married women I spoke with indicated that the division of labor is never blatantly mapped out but, rather, is something that evolves after various discussions (i.e., fights) with their partner. Typically, each team player brings in some money and does the specific household chores that he or she naturally gravitates toward (my husband usually cooks, while I do the dishes, for instance). Or one player has such perfectionistic expectations toward the way a certain chore is done that he or she insists on taking responsibility for that one; for example, Alexis, 27, of San Antonio, Texas, requires a well-made bed, and therefore she has designated that task for herself. Her husband, by the way, has a dishwasher fixation, insisting that the door remain locked when the dishes are clean and unlocked if there is any hint of grime inside. So in their household he manages dish duty.

As you and your husband begin to establish your particular roles in the marital merger, don't be shocked if you find yourselves frustrated with the process of delegation. Chores are one of the biggest sources of contention among newlyweds. For one thing, both you and your husband enter the partnership with preexisting ideas of what it takes to maintain a household. Each of you likely managed your previous homes in accordance with your own individual tolerance for mess and clutter. What's more, you both came to the merger with specific timelines for when you thought certain household tasks should be done and with what degree of vigor. This is particularly hard for marriages in which one partner is a slacker and the other is of Germanic descent.

These individual ideals often clash when, say, one of you feels the other isn't doing a fair share of laundry or one of you is maniacal about turning the home into a sterilized clutter-free zone. Or if one of you constantly "forgets" to put his dirty clothes in the hamper. To add to the problem, many women tend to take on the larger share of work when it comes to chores. Due partly to our socialization and partly to habit, taking on the bulk of household duties—unless, of course, you and your mate have agreed that's fair—will do your marriage no good.

Selena, 34, of New York, New York, discovered this soon after she got married and willingly took on the burden of doing laundry, cleaning, shopping, and paying bills—in addition to working full time. Eventually, she says, that resulted in resentment. For her the solution lay in letting her husband do his share of chores in his own timeline, even though it drove her crazy because it took him longer to do things. She likes to get chores done so she can relax, while he prefers to lounge around first.

A fair and equitable solution to the division of labor is key during the first year of marriage. Without one, you or your mate will begin to feel as though the balance of power is off, that one of you is acting as CEO and the other is secretary or janitor. In marriage, having an equal stake in the way your house is managed is critical to the happiness of everyone involved. The key points to get on the table in the division of labor negotiation are (1) determining what each of you desires in terms of cleanliness and clutter, including how often you want to give the house a deep cleaning as opposed to spot checks and everyday tidying, and (2) what each of you will take on in order to effect these desires. It also doesn't hurt to discuss how you'll handle the delicate issue of what to do when one of you begins to slack off on your chores or slips into doing a half-assed job. Alexis and her husband, for instance, went through a phase they call "Whose Job Is More Stressful?" During this phase they decided that whoever's job was more taxing during a particular time got to slack off on household chores. Problems arose, though, when they both felt zapped by the demands of their careers. As with managing time, tackling the division of labor issue requires a keen aptitude in communicating your needs and then working out a compromise. So, last but not least, let's discuss these two critical skills for managing marriage.

negotiation

There's nothing like the business of marriage to put your verbal aptitude to the test. There is simply so much to talk about, so much to negotiate. In fact, I can't think of one thing in marriage that doesn't require negotiation. Finances, chores, sex (as in what to do when you want it and he doesn't), how much time to spend with the folks, how much time to spend with each other, where to go on vacation, what to have for dinner—*everything* requires negotiation. But there are certain ways of communicating with your spouse that yield success. Let's recap the two basic principles of negotiation, shall we?

basic pinciple #1: communication is a two-way street

Before two parties can begin to negotiate the issue at stake, each must first be able to articulate his or her wants, needs, and feelings. This is not an easy task for many individuals, especially if expressing your desires goes directly against those of your partner and, therefore, has the potential of provoking a fight or hurting feelings. In fact, many couples avoid expressing themselves just so they can avoid conflict.

In marriage as in business, avoiding conflict is the worst thing a couple can do. Family therapists call such practices "avoidance" or "withdrawal," and they say it's the number one predictor of divorce. The reason is that avoiding conflict deprives you of the opportunity to build good negotiation skills with your partner. These skills are critical in the event you are both faced with unexpected stress: You lose your job, you have a surprise pregnancy, or an unreliable family member needs to borrow money. Unless you and your mate plan to live in a bubble, you will come face-to-face with unexpected stress at some point in your marriage, so you need to know how to handle differences. Otherwise, you'll crack when you most need the skills and strength to negotiate.

Expressing yourself does not mean you must suggest a solution to the issue you are grappling with; that comes later in the negotiating phase. The first step is simply to let your partner know how you feel: "In situations such as *(fill in the blank),* I feel *(fill in the blank: angry/hurt/lonely/ exhausted/happy)."* Or "When you *(fill in the blank),* it makes me feel . . ." Here's an example to try on for size: "When you throw your clothes on the back of a chair instead of putting them in the hamper, it first makes me angry and frustrated, and then I start feeling depressed." Here's another one: "When we're talking about how to spend our savings, I feel anxious and ignored."

Helen, 33, of Washington, D.C., learned during her first year of marriage that she often worried more about her husband's needs than about expressing her own; this then led to a breakdown in their communication. "My husband would ask where I wanted to go to dinner, and I'd say, 'I don't know. What would you like?' This would lead to a highly irritating conversation until I'd blurt out 'Mexican food!' I learned that my husband much prefers when I say what I want. And that makes me happier, too."

It is also important when it comes to building up strong communication skills with your mate to listen to him without challenging or criticizing him (as in "I can't believe you feel that way!") and without adding comments, opinions, or judgments (as in "Maybe if you did such-and-such, things would get better at work"). Such suggestions are appropriate later, during the negotiation part. For now your job is simply to listen, to give your partner a chance to vent, talk, and express his full range of emotions—anger, joy, fear, frustration, jealousy.

Listening to your husband is often hard to do, especially if what he is saying irks, scares, or challenges you. That's where your skills in listening are really put to the test. The ultimate verbal response to listening is "Uh-huh." Even better, follow this up by paraphrasing what he just said: "So let me get this straight. You think I overreact when we get into disagreements about money." When your husband confirms what you've reiterated, proper listening etiquette dictates that you respond objectively (as opposed to defensively). "Hmmm . . ." or "Interesting . . ." are two such responses. You may disagree with what he says, but you can't disagree with his feelings. And that's what is important for him to know right now.

Sometimes when I feel the need to comment on whatever it is my husband is saying that I thoroughly disagree with, I bite my tongue. Literally. Biting my tongue is the only way I can prevent myself from interrupting him, getting defensive, and then saying things I will regret later. Granted, I'm not always able to hold back, but the tongue biting helps sometimes. Other times I sit on my hands, which tend to fly automatically to my forehead as though I'm experiencing a terrible migraine when we get into a heated discussion. Though this gesture isn't meant to stifle discussion, I have learned that it's a nonverbal way of discouraging my husband from fully airing his views. With hands firmly locked in a defenseless position, I make an effort to repeat what my husband said so I can get it straight in my own mind. The truth is, repeating what I've just heard typically calms me, because it helps me separate my husband's feelings from what I might otherwise feel is a personal attack on my character.

At times, listening is even harder than expressing yourself, but it is vital to being able to negotiate differences. If you don't understand exactly where your husband is coming from, if you don't fully grasp his dreams, desires, wants, feelings, fears, or general malcontent with whatever is being discussed, then the two of you won't be able to come up with a solution that you both can live with. Besides, feeling understood is the glue to intimacy. If you and your mate can get this communication skill down, you can negotiate almost anything.

basic principle #2: argue for a solution, don't fight to win

The second principle for successful negotiation is coming up with solutions to conflicts without shutting down emotionally or creating power struggles that go against the nature of a successful partnership. Once each of you airs your feelings, it's time to begin the talks.

The first rule of negotiation is for you and your partner to agree right off the bat that the goal is to figure out a solution for the time being, rather than solve all your problems and end world hunger, too, while you're at it. This will remove some of the pressure of the argument as well as help both of you focus on the healthy goal of collaboration rather than on the sickly goal of trying to prove a point or fighting to win an argument. Easier said than done, I know.

One of the hardest things about negotiating is separating your emotions from the problems. When discussions get heated—and they will—it's vital that each of you knows how to calm yourself down so that you can think clearly enough to focus on a solution rather than shutting down or slamming doors. Taking deep breaths is one trick I practice. Not only does it give me a chance to refocus instead of shut down, but it also helps trigger the relaxation mechanism so I don't get so riled up. Other women I spoke with suggest taking a short break from your partner—even if that involves just a walk around the block—to clear your mind in the thick of the argument and refocus on the goal of getting through the disagreement and working toward a solution. My husband's stepmother once told me that there was no argument that couldn't be solved with a glass of wine and a brisk run around the block. She has a point: When you are tipsy and physically refreshed, you're less on the offense, and it's easier to work out a solution.

Selena agrees that the most successful way to argue is to wait until the intensity of the emotion passes, and then talk. "I don't respond well to yelling. I shut down," she says. "My husband comes from a family of screamers. That's his style. We both have to practice new ways of communicating. I have to remember not to say anything I'll regret in anger. I keep it at the front of my mind that this is my best friend whom I adore and don't want to hurt."

Invoking humor is another trick for diffusing stress and anger, and it also sets you up for better interaction. My husband and I, for instance, have developed a recurring joke that deals with my apprehension concerning his driving style, which I occasionally find too aggressive for my nerves. When my husband is behind the wheel, we sometimes get into an argument about how he handles certain traffic incidents, such as being cut off while driving on the freeway. While I prefer a quick angry beep in protest, followed by careful defensive measures, such as steering clear of the offending driver, my husband prefers the prolonged honk coupled with repeated high-beam flashes and various other punishing acts, such as riding on the offending car's tail or flipping off the culprit. I have to say in my normally mild-mannered husband's defense that he's an exceptional driver and has never been in a car accident since I've known him, while I've been in two—one of which destroyed the front end of his prized red 1967 Porsche. Let's just say we have different driving styles, and it's been a source of contention between us.

At first I handled my anxiety about his aggressive driving by screaming at him—"GET A GRIP ON YOUR FRIGGIN' TESTOSTERONE AND DRIVE MORE DEFENSIVELY!" or a similar verbal response. But that always left us both angry and bitter as we drove on toward our destination in stony silence. Then one time when he was cut off and attempting to flash the high beams at the offending vehicle, the windshield wipers came on instead. Rather than screech at him to slow down and chill out, all the while pointing out how his flustered state caused the wipers to go on unexpectedly—a potential hazard to our safety, no doubt—I started laughing about the wipers and the water that was squirting all over our windshield. And, lo and behold, instead of his getting even more flustered and defensive, he cracked up, too.

Since then the wipers have become a running joke whenever we feel the stirrings of road rage coming on. If ever he's driving and someone pisses him off, he flips on the windshield wipers, and we chuckle the incident away. (Of course I'm sure he doesn't do this when I'm not in the car, but that's his prerogative, I tell him, as I subtly remind him that aggressive maneuvers on the road could lead to accidents and that I really, really don't want to become a widow at age 31.) What I have noticed since the wipers incident is that he doesn't get nearly as upset by jerky drivers as he used to, and I don't get nearly as upset by his occasional high-beam F-you response to them. Laughter has been the key to our sanity on this issue. God bless the windshield wipers!

Amber also swears by the benefits of humor. When she

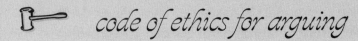

code of ethics for arguing

When arguing, there are certain fair and unfair tactics. What follows are some suggestions for proper negotiation when the topic becomes heated.

1. NO LOW BLOWS. For instance, instead of saying "You're a dickhead!" when angry at your mate, try "You're not being a team player." Leave personality inadequacies, such as being lazy or selfish, out of all verbal communication. Save these for your journal, which should be kept under lock and key.

2. STICK TO THE ISSUES AT STAKE. Do not bring up past problems or use examples from previous events that illustrate the point you're attempting to argue. This infuriates most people and will lead to defensiveness, which breaks down communication instead of helping to find a compromise.

3. AVOID INTERRUPTING. Nothing halts communication like interrupting. Silencing your partner's opinions only leads to shutting down.

4. REMEMBER THE LOVE. Never let yourself forget all the reasons that you respect your partner. One of the best ways I've found of getting out of the anger mode and into the negotiation mode is simply to say, "I'm sorry I hurt your feelings. I was out of line." Note: I don't apologize for my opinions or back down from my point of view. I simply express my regret that whatever I've done or said has upset my husband. My regret is genuine. Reminding your partner that you respect him and want to work toward peace will motivate both of you to negotiate.

gets angry, her instinct is to want to break things. During one fight with her husband, she grabbed a chair with the intention of smashing it. When her husband saw the potential scenario, he said, "Okay, you want to break something. . . . Wait—let me get my cell phone," which made them both crack up and then refocus on the problem rather than their rage.

Once you have your emotions in check and your points of view clearly expressed, the next step in conflict resolution is to chisel away at the issues until you come up with a solution. Here's the reality: In healthy negotiations each person relinquishes some part of an ideal solution to come up with something suitable to both. That may mean an entirely new solution, or it could mean that each one compromises his and her ideologies bit by bit. Continuing to express your feelings and views throughout this brokering will help ensure that the compromise is one you both can live with.

As you talk about the issues, keep in mind that not all conflicts are solvable. When you come to a standstill or when you're simply too tired to continue negotiating, just agree that you and your partner will disagree. Then give your lover a long kiss and tell him that you're sorry if you hurt his feelings because you love him very much. You may be surprised how easily this simple act can melt the tension. Finally, get on with your life. You may find that after a day or two the issue at stake provokes less and less passion. If, however, the issue is ongoing, seek help from a mediator (that is, a family counselor). All of us can use a little professional guidance now and then.

*t*he new you

Entering the state of matrimony is a bit like entering a foreign country where your usual way of life and even your identity often experience a brief period of readjustment. As you do when you travel, you'll be acclimating to a new culture—one that combines your previous lifestyle with that of your mate. The adaptation process typically entails a number of changes.

For starters, you and your travel partner (i.e., husband) will be learning a new language called Marriagespeak, which finds its linguistic roots in those intimate communication skills we talked about in the last chapter. This is a terribly difficult vernacular to master, by the way, but not one that can't be learned through rigorous practice. While exploring the nuances of this new terrain and becoming ensconced in the culture of marriage, you'll quickly pick up the slang, including cutesy nicknames for each other, such as Babycakes, that no one else (hopefully) will overhear you utter.

Once you obtain your passport (that marriage certificate I keep mentioning), you and your husband will gradually begin to adapt to each other's lifestyles and adopt each other's mannerisms, intonations, and jokes. Your husband will introduce you to the exotic new foods that make up his daily diet (imported beer comes to mind), as will you to him. Your exercise schedule and social life may also change due to your new marital commitments and the additional stresses that go along with cohabitation, all of which may prevent you from prioritizing the treadmill. About 95 percent of women even change their name in an attempt to fully acclimate themselves to the new culture of matrimony.

As when living abroad, your political views may veer slightly due to the influence of your significant other's worldview. Molly, 31, of Philadelphia, Pennsylvania, recalls that her apolitical husband became more interested in politics after they got married because of her passion for women's issues. His birthday gift to her was registering to vote. That he actually voted Democratic in the election that followed soon after was beyond her wildest dreams. Once you've properly acclimated to the initial culture shock of marriage, everything about your past life may begin to feel foreign.

Occasionally you'll get homesick for the old world's customs, such as chilling out in front of the TV whenever you like, spontaneously deciding to see a movie at the theater down the street at 10 P.M., or having your girlfriends over for pre-party primping without having to ask your husband to hang out in the basement for a while. You may even get frustrated because your previous lifestyle and once-predictable home life is now occupied by a second party who screams "Yes!" and "Foul!!" at the TV when his favorite football team is playing, making you feel slightly out of place and even unsure of how to spend your time when both of you are just hanging out at home. But the enriched experience of living in the new marital culture— which *does* change your old habits if I haven't made that clear enough yet—outweighs the things you'll miss.

As when living abroad, the culture shock of marriage typically lasts a few months to a year. Then you gradually adapt to the subtle, unexpected changes in your identity, including your looks, life goals, sense of autonomy, and possibly even your name.

mrs. who?

Personally, the toughest decision I had with the entire wedding/marriage cultural initiation was whether or not to change my last name, and it wasn't just because of the dastardly paperwork associated with the whole process, as described in the previous chapter. My angst was rooted in the fact that my name *was* my identity. I had been Julia Hillen Bourland for thirty years, and during the last five I'd managed to get my byline into a variety of national magazines, on a weekly sex column in the *San Francisco Chronicle*, and on the cover of my first book. Call me egotistical, but when magazine editors contacted me for a quote in an article about women's self-esteem or the like, I wanted the quote to say, "According to Bourland . . ." What's more, Bourland was an *unusual* cognomen. If I changed it to my husband's more ubiquitous name, Chambers, the Bourland bloodline would be one generation closer to extinction.

At the same time I wanted my husband and me to share the same name. To me *that* was meaningful and symbolic and sexy. Becoming a Chambers, in my mind, would be a constant reminder that my husband had chosen me to be his best friend, lifelong lover, and family. In a public sense, sharing the same last name legitimized the fact that we were married (an outdated societal view, perhaps, but true in many parts of the country). What's more, having two separate last names begged the question of what to do when we eventually started a family—give our children all hyphenated last names? That seemed cruel.

My husband, who's about as liberal as men come, understood my dilemma; he, too, strongly identified with his surname (his nickname *is* his last name) and therefore wouldn't consider changing his to mine. But he would understand if I didn't take his—even though he hoped I would (which was great of him to say, but he still put the onus of the decision on me). We joked about combining our names to create a new one: Bourbers or Chambourland. But those seemed like odd throwback solutions from the 1970s and didn't help with the family lineage propagation we suddenly felt was important.

So we came up with a compromise: I'd legally change my last name to Chambers if he would legally add Bourland to his as a second middle name. For now I would continue to use Bourland professionally (which is why you see it on the cover of this book). When we have kids, we'll give them all the middle name Bourland and go by the family name of Chambers; this will keep my name circulating, if only as a middle name, for at least one more generation. Then if our kids don't care about immortalizing Bourland, I'll, let it rest in peace.

It sounds confusing, but the duo-name scenario has been working well for me. In fact, I kind of like having two names—one social and one that's all business. I don't have trouble separating the two or remembering which name to use under which circumstance (one of my original concerns). In fact, I highly recommend experimenting with two names to anyone who's grappling with the issue. Laurie Scheuble, Ph.D., senior lecturer of sociology at Penn State who has written on the subject, has a name for women like me: "situational last-name users." According to her research, about 25 percent of women these days go back and forth between using their maiden and married names.

There are several reasons to consider maintaining an element of your birth name within marriage—whether you take the situational approach, as I have done, or shift your maiden name to middle-name status or hyphenate the two last names, which only about 1 percent of women do. Of these, many eventually end up dropping the hyphen and taking their husband's name because of the hassle of constantly having to spell out their name and the frustration of having to redo all the resulting paperwork errors.

Scheuble points out that changing one's name breaks down social and professional networks that women build up in life. Former colleagues, associates, and long-lost friends who aren't aware that you have gotten married or who don't know your husband's last name, for instance, won't be able to track you down. In the South and Northeast, she adds, last names are especially critical for ties to land and identity—something women need to consider. If you have siblings, it will be strange to lose the last-name connection you share with them. And if your name reveals a cultural or ethnic affiliation, you'll have to consider how giving that up for, say, a name like Smith will affect your sense of heritage and cultural affinity.

There's also the issue of bunking with tradition. Women who choose not to change their name may have to deal with disbelief and even disapproval from traditionalist relatives, friends, and even strangers. One woman I interviewed told me that the phone company didn't believe she was married because she didn't have the same last name as her husband; therefore, it wouldn't make changes in their service, which was under his name. Muriel, 30, of Portland, Oregon, who did not change her name after getting hitched, clashed with the tradition as early as her wedding day. After the ceremony, instead of being introduced with fanfare at the reception as Mr. and Mrs. So-and-so, the DJ announced their entry with something like "Ladies and gentlemen, please welcome Muriel and Richard!" It was comical to them and some of the guests since they were Muriel and Richard before the wedding, too.

Deborah, 30, of Santa Cruz, California, and her husband also face social flack for going against the grain of tradition. Both decided to hyphenate each other's name once they were married. As a result, their friends tease her husband about his new name and being "under the ball and chain of his wife's wishes," which makes Deborah feel guilty and then defensive about their mutual decision to hyphenate.

Of course, not all women grapple with the name-change question. Some know long before they meet their soul mate that they'll change their name when married regardless of what that last name might be. Allison, 27, of Dallas, Texas, for instance, hated her last name since she was a child and learned from tittering tourists that her name in German was slang for "fuck." She couldn't wait to get married so she could change it.

Chloe, 26, of Santa Barbara, Califorinia, also never cared much for her maiden name because it rhymed with her first name. She also didn't have a good relationship with her father, so there wasn't much sentimental value at stake when the opportunity arose to change it. She was so enthusiastic about taking on her husband's name that she went to the Social Security Administration office to get a new card even before the wedding. (They denied her application, by the way, because she didn't have a marriage certificate yet.) Initially, Dara, 27, of Tampa, Florida, kept her maiden name professionally and used her married name for everything else, but after a year or so she began to identify more with her married name and slowly phased out the old one. As she put it, "Before I got married, I thought that keeping my name would help me maintain my individual identity. But I found out that I didn't need a name to do that."

In the end, the choice is entirely personal, since there are no right or wrong reasons on which to base your decision. If you do opt to change your name, there are a few safety measures worth taking to ensure that you don't lose touch with former acquaintances: (1) Send an email and/or letter to everyone in your address book and Rolodex announcing your new name. If your email address is changing, too, include the new one as well so everyone can update your contact info in one swift, painless act. (2) List both your new and old names in your local phone directory. I pay about 80 cents a month for the double listing. It's worth it because my maiden name is tied to my livelihood. (3) Ask your alumni organizations—college and even high school, if you like—to list both your maiden and married names on alumni lists and referral databases. (4) Consider introducing the change in stages: Molly, for example, used her maiden name as a middle name professionally for about a year after she got married. That way, old clients were able to recognize her while getting used to the new surname, and new clients would get to know her by her new last name. When she switched jobs, she abandoned her maiden middle name on professional correspondences since her new colleagues wouldn't know the difference. Sonya, 29, of Tampa, Florida, took a similar approach; she waited until she and her husband moved from Chicago to Tampa to begin using her married last name. New acquaintances didn't know the difference.

the married look

Is there a signature look among wives of America? Not really, from what I gathered in my interviewing—except, perhaps, that revealing metal band so many of us wear on our left ring finger. What is more a factor than marriage, in terms of our looks, is our age. And it just so happens that many of us tie the knot right around the time we begin to show our age (in our late twenties and early thirties).

Still, there is a visual myth (marriage equals frumpy) that many of us desperately wish to debunk after tying the knot. Very few of us want to be seen as "the girl who let herself go after getting hitched." And so, not long after we return from our honeymoon (a few pounds heavier, no doubt, from all that dining and wining and, well, let's just say lounging around in bed), many of us can't help but take a critical assessment of our looks.

It's my theory that this sudden need to take inventory of our body and current style is a reaction to all the changes we are facing in our new role of life partner. Because we are female and have been socialized to correlate our looks with our self-worth, body image often becomes a subject of obsession during times of uncertainty (which is one reason that our twenties were so fraught with the body image blues, as were our teens). The body reassessment may also be partly the result of being suddenly expelled from the status of Sexually Available Woman. That permanent removal may trigger some conflict in self-esteem—especially if you're the type of girl who thrives on the notion of being sexually desired by the male population.

The lesson here, of course, is that our looks should not define our identity, but I could write that a thousand times and *still* wish to lose five pounds. And here's another lesson that many of you will learn during the first year of marriage if you didn't already pick it up in your premarital state: Your husband loves you no matter what you look like, and this knowledge grows stronger the longer you are together. It will give rise to a sense of worth that is entirely unrelated to your looks. If your husband does not love you because your looks change after you get married (and they *will*, given time), then—and I hate to break it to you this way— he really doesn't love you. He loves the image of you. That's not to say, however, that your husband might not prefer one look over another or wish that you would dress up for him or shed a few pounds. There's nothing wrong with his having opinions about your looks as long as he is gentle and complimentary and very supportive when expressing them.

That being said, I thought I would mention three areas in which your looks might change during the first year: your hair, your weight, and your style. Many women experience these alterations after tying the knot, and I figured I'd bring them up so you wouldn't confuse them with your evolving identity. After all, they are simply physical modifications.

your hair

The most universal change women make following the wedding has to do with hair. Many newly hitched girls get a radical new hairstyle following the big day to define a new look for their married persona. One reason may be that in future pictures they'll be able to distinguish between the pre- and post-wedding eras. But many of you also have grown tired of the style you have been growing and perfecting for months leading up to the wedding and are ripe for a drastic change.

I had been growing out my tresses for about a year prior to my wedding, but my need for a new hairstyle came from someplace far deeper than a year's worth of hair boredom. You see, I had had the exact same hairstyle for the entire ten years between college and marriage—a blunt cut falling just below the shoulders. The greatest amount of variation I allowed my locks was alternating between wearing it down (on the rare occasion I was motivated to blow-dry it) or scrunching it up into a low-rider ponytail. So three weeks after our return from New Zealand, I marched into the salon and instructed my fabulous hairdresser, Ernest, to chop it off, which he did with supreme finesse. I've never had a more radical change in my look (apart from those perm experimentations in the 80s), and I loved it.

By the way, your husband may begin to experiment with facial hair during the honeymoon or after the wedding. It seems that men, too, are eager for a change in style to mark their change in status.

your weight

Another alteration in look that many of us, unfortunately, witness following the wedding is a subtle (or drastic, worst-case scenario) increase in weight. Granted, not all women gain the average five to ten pounds during the first year, so don't start freaking out just yet. If you're worried about putting on a little extra weight after tying the knot, there are certainly ways to keep your body size and shape close to its pre-wedding state. The trick is to recognize all the factors going against you and then work out a prevention plan ahead of time.

The post-wedding weight gain typically stems from a variety of things. Those of you who jumped on the *crash diet du jour* during the weeks prior to your wedding in an attempt to drop ten pounds, so you'd look svelte in your wedding gown, will undoubtedly be experiencing a metabolism funk that will actually cause you to *gain* weight faster than ever as soon as you start eating normally again (which is usually during your honeymoon).

Did I just mention metabolism? More discouraging news: Those of you over the age of 25 will be concurrently wrestling with a slowing metabolism in general, making it harder to maintain your weight without eating less or tripling your exercise routine (which is a cruel joke since our metabolism rise typically corresponds with our career rise, leaving less time for working out). The metabolism hike is, of course, Mother Nature's cruelty, not a by-product of marriage. But the longer you're married, the more the metabolism factor will play a role, so I thought I'd mention it now to prepare you.

Another reason some women put on a few pounds after marriage is that their lifestyles go through a reorganization—especially those who were not living with their fiancé before marriage. Many find, for instance, that their daily rhythm adjusts to accommodate more quality time with their husband (see the previous chapter for more details). While in the past you may have religiously hit the gym after work every day, you may now opt to skip it when you're working late if it means that you can squeeze in an extra hour of bonding with your mate or even have dinner together—which brings me to the food issue. (See how all these things are connected?)

Many of us witness a change in diet once we get married, a phenomenon often directly related to the weight gain issue. Again, if you lived with your husband before marriage, your diet has most likely already made the necessary adjustments to co-dining. If you're new to living together, here's what typically happens: Dinner for two often becomes more elaborate after marriage, complete with wine and dessert. It's my suspicion that the upscaled dining routine stems from the fact that you and your mate have suddenly upgraded your entire kitchen, thanks to all your wedding presents, enabling you to create masterpiece meals when in the past all you could manage with a pot and a steak knife was pasta and garlic bread. The increased emphasis on evening dining may also come from a marriage-inspired desire to have an "authentic family dinner" every night, complete with two types of vegetables—the way you ate when you were growing up (or, more commonly, the way you wish you ate when you were growing up).

To add to the complexity is the issue of what to eat during dinner now that you and your mate are buying groceries for two and preparing full sit-down meals instead of gulping down Top Ramen from a microwavable container on your way out to some party or art gallery opening where you hoped to meet that special someone. If you are anything like me, you ate cereal for dinner prior to living with your mate. Though nutritionally inept, such meals do have the bonus of keeping your weight down—something I realized only after I moved in with Lawrence (who, by the way, is a fabulous cook) and started eating real food every night like a normal person. Consequently, I put on eight or so pounds within the first year that we lived together.

Not only might your dinner menu change after moving in with your mate, but so might the proportions you choose to consume. It took me three years to figure out that I really didn't have to match what my husband ate every night. Granted, I *wanted* to because I have a healthy appetite and we always tend to overestimate how much food to cook, creating leftovers that I'd rather did not rot in the fridge. But when I do match his portions and cozy up with more than one glass of wine or beer per meal, as he does without a thought to the diameter of his waist, my hips start spreading like wildfire. It's so unfair! And speaking of all things unfair, why is it that when some men don't work out, they *lose* weight?

If you are new to co-dining, these issues will eventually work themselves out, and you'll find a balance regarding the food issue. If you're like me, you'll learn how to eat healthier (though I have to admit that whenever my husband goes out of town on business, I tend to get decadent and eat like old times—appeasing my appetite with something sweet around 8 P.M. and often skipping dinner altogether).

Alicia, 34, of Kailua, Hawaii, notes that her eating habits have come full circle in the five years she's been married. Originally a food purist subsisting mainly on tofu and rice, she felt lost when her husband brought chips and fried food into the house, and *distressed* when he ordered chow mein at Chinese restaurants. These items didn't complement her way of eating. Eventually she saw how content her husband was with what he ate and began trying some of his foods. Now, however, she says she's gravitating toward her original eating styles, trying to strike a balance between the his and her diets.

Jackie, 30, of El Dorado Hills, California, who is a vegetarian, and her husband, who is not, came up with a different solution: They eat separately—she at the table sitting down, and he standing at the stove while he's cooking. They figure they'll work on the family meal concept when they have kids. For now, the separate dining suits them. They do the bonding thing later on, after dinner.

To sum up the weight and food issue, my advice is to

realize that cohabitation may bring changes in your eating and exercising routines, which may have an affect on your weight. If you're concerned, be vigilant about staying on course during the first year of marriage when you will be particularly vulnerable to all the adjustments and changes taking place in your current lifestyle.

your style

One final area of your looks that may change during the first year of marriage is your style, specifically your wardrobe and the degree of primping you choose to engage in each day. To generalize the phenomenon, here's what you might expect: Your wardrobe may become slightly less current, and the degree of primping you engage in each morning may dwindle. Clearly, not every married woman experiences the downgrade in style, and you may be one who defies the odds. Hey, more power to you! But I did hear about the phenomenon enough in my interviewing to deem it worth mentioning.

The most common explanation I came across for style relaxation was that a girl's earthy husband preferred her *au naturel*. And his acceptance of her natural beauty was all she needed to refrain from the exhausting work of appearing hip and beautiful in public. Dara, for example, says her husband seems to think she looks the same whether she spends five or fifty minutes getting ready. So she tends to wear no makeup and lets her hair hang as it will.

My husband falls into the earthy husband category as well. He has on more than one occasion threatened to de-wire all my bras! As a result of his natural persuasions, I have come to care a little bit less about looking stylistically current—until I'm around all my hip girlfriends, that is, and then I go on a frenzied shopping spree to keep up with the times. But I digress.

Another common cause of the downgraded look some married women find themselves in has to do with money. Once you enter marriage, many of you will find yourselves designating a portion of your salary to unprecedented "marital money goals"—usually big-ticket items that you and your husband want to save for, such as a house, a baby, or a change in career (which could mean a drop in income). What this has to do with your style: You'll likely have less money to spend on keeping your wardrobe current.

The last reason your style may change after getting married has to do with your confidence. Frankly, you will probably care less about your physical image because you will no longer be desperate to find a mate. You have found one. What's more, the love you feel for your life partner (adoration expands exponentially once you tie the knot) often replaces many of the emotional insecurities you had prior to finding love, insecurities that led you to fixate on your looks and constantly update your style to maximize your ability to attract attention.

That being said, I would like to mention one thing that the downgrading of style might do to your identity. It could put a damper on your sense of sex appeal, which is just as alive and kick-ass in hitched girls as it is in their single sisters. The truth is, it is extremely important to feel good about your sex appeal within marriage. What's more, it is *critical* to your sex life that you feel sexy and attractive around your husband, even if he doesn't notice a difference between one look and another. So if wearing the latest styles and wearing makeup gives you a sense of sexiness, don't let this aspect of yourself be denied by a back-to-nature husband (or a shrinking checking account).

Your job as a married woman is to nurture your sense of sexiness so that you feel attractive. If you don't, you may constantly need affirmation about your looks from your husband, which most likely will put an unfair strain on him—especially if he's the type who really does prefer you *au naturel*. Dara, whose husband, you may recall, doesn't notice her primping attempts, leading her to slack off, says she has recently made an effort to primp on a day-to-day basis. Doing so makes her feel better about her looks.

marriage: the stabilizer

I have some fabulous news to share with you: Marriage is a boon for a girl's self-esteem (unless you have a selfish, spiteful husband, of course, in which case the opposite is probably true). Since I purposely limited my interviews for this book to women who are in role-model marriages, it's no surprise that they all spoke of the boost in confidence they experienced after tying the knot. Avery, 33, of New York, New York, is a good example: "I've become a much stronger person since I got married. I feel more comfortable and self-confident. I've always believed that commitment sets you free, and in this case, committing to my husband freed up so much of my psyche. I no longer worried about if a guy called or not, or the larger question: Will I ever find my soul mate? I knew I had. This commitment freed up a whole part of my life and left more space for me to focus on other areas."

Most of these women also point to the fact that marriage has given them a live-in supporter, their husband, who has encouraged them to take new risks and discover the other parts of their identity that were formerly buried or disregarded during their search for love. The new sense of stability and permanence that goes along with marriage leads many women to discover parts of themselves that previously hadn't had a chance to develop or unfold. What follows are three of the most common awakenings.

the professional awakening

There appear to be two camps in the career arena following marriage. Some women experience an explosion of professional ambition once the search for a mate and wedding planning has ended, allowing them to focus on their career goals in a way they couldn't before. The security of their husband's income, plus his unwavering emotional support and inherent masculine quality of going after what he wants, has even influenced some of these women to initiate professional risks they wouldn't have taken had their livelihood been entirely dependent on their own salary. (This works both ways, by the way. Many women I spoke with have acted as the stable financial provider in marriage, allowing their husbands the opportunity to seek more satisfying careers. In an ideal marriage each partner gets a shot at this.)

Mandy, 32, of San Francisco, California, who is an accountant for a software company, has also begun the first steps of a career change since marriage. Having always dreamed of becoming a jewelry designer, she has started taking classes and spending her weekends designing jewelry—a professional move that will result in a huge cut in pay and therefore was too risky to pursue without the stability of her husband's income. Candace, 34, of New York, New York, has also taken professional risks she might not have if she was single. An actor, Candace had always supported her creative career with administrative jobs here and there. Gradually those jobs began to leave her less time for acting and writing. Once she and her husband tied the knot, her mate convinced her to focus solely on her acting ambitions.

The second camp of women going through a professional awakening has quite the opposite experience. These women, due to marriage, come to a realization that their careers are not the defining point of their identity and not what is ultimately important to them in life. Dara, a successful magazine writer, for instance, says her career seems to be less important because she has realized there's more to life than work. While she continues to write for a living, she has begun to reevaluate her career goals, struggling to figure out her dreams and ambitions. For her the three years following her wedding have served as a time for her to figure out who she is and where she wants to go in life—keeping in mind that her husband has to fit into that plan.

Paula, 31, of Spokane, Washington, also experienced a shift in career ambitions since tying the knot. Several years before she met her husband, she realized she might never marry, so her goal in life was to become a professor. "I still wanted children at some point, so I figured a good profession for a single mother was that of professor," she says. She began a Ph.D. program. When she eventually met her soul mate and then married him three years ago, her goals shifted: "Getting a Ph.D. became less important to me. A greater priority was to live in the city where I live now— something that would have to change if I wanted to be a professor." So for now she has put her Ph.D. on hold and is working for the local government as a civil engineer.

Barbara, 30, of Staten Island, New York, who is currently in a medical residency program, made a similar career reevaluation following her marriage. She says that thoughts of family life in the future have primarily curbed her ambitions. If she wasn't married and so aware of her biological clock, she says she'd be much more aggressive about getting a fellowship and a specialty in her residency program. Nina, 30, of San Francisco, California, also altered her career path for love. The day after she got engaged, she received an acceptance letter from a business school across the country. Her fiancé, who was in the midst of making partner at his law firm, told her he couldn't move. Not knowing what to do, Nina flew to the school's welcome weekend and had the following epiphany: It's much easier to find a good job in Silicon Valley than it is to find a good man. So she got a deferment for B-school and started planning the wedding. A month later she was promoted to vice president at her job; she began making more money than her husband, the law partner, which goes to show that there is never just one clear-cut road to career (or marital) success.

Molly, who admits she's a workaholic, also modified her career path after getting married. After she and her husband married, her career became a source of contention between them; he felt that working until 10 P.M. every night was no longer acceptable now that they were married. (They had lived together before getting hitched, and working late hours apparently wasn't a problem then.) "My husband felt lonely and abandoned," says Molly. "It became a big issue in our marriage—so much so that I left consulting. I decided that I needed to put my relationship first. Initially I was resentful that my husband was asking me to make that change. But now I have a better balance between work and life. I'm gaining quality time with my husband, *and* I'm skyrocketing to the top of my new career."

the nesting syndrome awakening

The nesting syndrome is a foreign and slightly disconcerting desire to snuggle up inside the house, ideally with no one else but your new husband, instead of running around town five nights a week as you did premarriage. Part of this syndrome is due, I believe, to that commitment you just made. Many of you are still high from your wedding ceremony and want to indulge in marital domesticity, getting to know how the role of husband is playing out on that man with whom you exchanged lifelong vows. The role of life partner, which has recently been added to your repertoire of personal responsibilities, may also be causing you to slow down and chill out. (When women take on too many roles, all of them become compromised.)

It's also my belief that part of the draw to domesticity is due to the recent influx of wedding gifts—elaborate cookware, delicate china, fine wine—that makes hanging out around the home and cooking elaborate meals for each other far more novel than it used to be. If you and your mate moved following your marriage, the blank canvas of your new abode may also be influencing your penchant for all things domestic. I admit, it hit me. Not long after our return from New Zealand, I started fantasizing about becoming a housewife. I imagined myself wearing post–World War II–type dresses while baking bread, growing a garden, and hanging the laundry out to dry on a clothesline! Granted, part of my fantasizing could have been due to the fact that I was told I'd be laid off from my Web site producer job within the next three months. I was obviously looking for a role to fall back on during the recession-doomed job market I was about to face. Still, the domestic dreaming had me stunned in the beginning, because I've always been so quick to identify with my career before any-thing domestic. Plus, I've *never* considered myself a home-body. Actually, this fantasy has very little to do with my evolving role of wife. It's really all about sex, but I'll explain that in the next chapter.

Another reason many of you might be feeling particu-larly wifey (in the traditional sense) is that everyone is ask-ing you when you and your new husband are going to start having babies. These inquisitions then force you to ponder the question yourself. And since many of us are waiting until the final hour of our prime fertility years before tying the knot, that damn biological clock may also be ticking loudly in our ears.

Here's a bit of advice on dealing with the nesting syn-drome: Enjoy it! This may be the first time you've allowed domesticity into your personality, and you just may discover how stabilizing a little bit of home life can be. Soon enough the real world kicks back in, with work, friendships, the gym, and your husband all beckoning for more of your time. Gradually you'll find a balance when it comes to man-aging all the various aspects of your life.

the spiritual awakening

Yes, you, too, may have a spiritual awakening (of sorts), directly resulting from your recent marriage. Speaking for myself, I've noticed an explosion of emotions since my wed-ding. I tear up at *everything* that moves my spirit: beautiful music, a baby, an awe-inspiring view. The only way I can explain this awakening (forgive my gushing) is that I've entered a more heightened state of awareness, a state in which my emotional capacity is a hundred times more raw and exposed than before. I attribute this directly to my relationship with my husband, a relationship that, through the security of marriage, has given me the opportunity and courage to feel more than I've ever allowed myself to feel. And that has awakened parts of my soul that have been dormant for years.

Maya, 32, of Portland, Oregon, noticed an urge to nurture her spiritual side after marriage, too. One way she expressed this was by organizing a Seder for her husband and friends for the first time without family. She says she wanted to make Judaism her and her husband's own tradition. Her husband, by the way, initially opposed the feast, associating Passover with childhood memories of unbearable boredom and sitting hours at the table while adults yammered on and on. But once they started the ceremony, he was the one who wanted to follow the traditions by the book, even criticizing her for skipping some of the readings. Maya also felt that carrying on family traditions—or modifying them to their own tastes, as she did—would keep them connected to their family's cultural background, which was important to her, especially if they were going to start making babies soon. (The baby-spirituality awakening, I gather from my girlfriends-turned-mothers, deserves a book of its own, so I'll just mention it here in passing.)

Mandy recalls a different type of spiritual awakening following marriage: a growing awareness of her own mortality. She noticed that she has become more cautious since tying the knot, saying that she's "freaked out about death more because I'm so happy." Faith, 29, of Los Angeles, California, had a similar feeling that began not long after her engagement. Her own happiness, she recalls, made her feel vulnerable to death. If her husband was driving and another driver decided to switch lanes right in front of him, he could get killed! (Remember those fatalistic thoughts during the engagement period?) Joseph Kelley, Ph.D., adjunct professor of religious studies and theology at Merrimack College in North Andover, Massachusetts, explains the phenomenon: "Marriage, by its nature, provokes general questions of transcendence and spirituality. The words 'until death do we part' open a box of questions about death and the afterlife. Marriage is often the first time young people confront their mortality—unless they have dealt with death before," he says. "Also, your singleness is dying in marriage. You're limiting yourself to one person for the rest of your life. When you encounter limitations, you encounter beginnings and endings. And those encounters often stir the spiritual."

your autonomy

Warning: I've been preparing you for this section because it's one of the hardest to handle in terms of how your identity will be affected during the first year of marriage. Rather than beat around the bush, I'm going to give it to you straight: In marriage you will have less autonomy. This means—to spell it out for you so there's no misunderstandings here—that you will have less independence in your life. Your personal goals will likely be affected and even altered by the new goals determined by you and your partner. These goals may not be the goals you would have chosen to strive for as a single woman. That's the reality of the nature of marriage, and it's one of the things that makes wedlock so hard for both women and men to deal with.

A loss of autonomy also means that you will have less privacy or alone time since your home will now be shared with your significant other (and, occasionally, his friends and family). His schedule and modus operandi will likely disrupt your premarriage lifestyle in which you had full control over every aspect of your life: when to eat and to sleep, how long to spend in the shower in the morning or talk on the phone at night. If you're the type who likes to wake up slowly in the morning but your husband is wide awake and chirpy the moment the alarm clock dings, adding his comments to every story he reads in the paper while you can barely manage to get coffee to lips, both of you will need to adjust. What's more, due to the nature of entering a lifelong partnership, you'll probably have to consult your husband on every decision you make—from the mundane (whether or not to take a weeklong vacation with your best girlfriend to Paris, which would mean having less vacation time to spend with him that year, not to mention the money factor if your finances are completely merged) to the profound (when the optimal time is to start a family or whether it is really wise to pursue a career change now). In other words, marriage inhibits you from making independent decisions. You will now need to consider your marital financial goals as well as your husband's feelings.

This loss of autonomy is, in my opinion, what distinguishes those of us who are married from those of us who are living together with our partners. The commitment to a lifelong partnership is what creates this divide (and also what makes the loss of autonomy a little easier to bear). But it's my belief that most problems in marriage—be it sharing money, divvying up chores, dealing with relatives—are all rooted in this struggle for autonomy. Many of us fear that we will lose our voice or that our opinions will be disregarded. The ugly truth is that we *will* lose our voice at times. And sometimes our opinions *will* play less of a role in the decisions we make with our husbands. But we'll regain our voice later, and other times our opinions will drive the course of our joint actions. Coming to terms with this reality (as opposed to denying it and continuing to live lives independent of each other) will help you deal with the loss you feel during the first year of matrimony. Worth mentioning here are the three secret ingredients for maintaining a fragment of autonomy within marriage: a mental sanctuary, girlfriends, and boundaries.

a mental sanctuary

In the last chapter I mentioned the importance of adopting a room of your own (or at least part of a room) so you can have a place to chill out and be creative and alone when you need it. Selena, 34, of New York City, New York, can attest to the importance of space: "My husband and I share a tiny living space. At first I felt intolerant when my husband was in my way in the morning. Every little thing he did annoyed me: He ate too loudly, was a slob, didn't clean up after himself. I missed my alone time, too. I was surprised at my intolerance, though. This was a man I loved more than anyone and took vows to share my life with. It made me fear that I was incapable of being in a relationship!"

In situations where lack of personal space is a real issue, getting out of the house may provide the mental freedom you need to feel independent. It may also give you space to dream about things you want to do and accomplish in life, without thinking about your husband's goals and the accomplishments you've decided to strive for as a team.

Many of the women I spoke with find this mental space while working out. Candace gets in touch with herself through dancing and going to the gym every morning (the dedication!). Kathleen, 27, of Portland, Oregon, who has a three-year-old daughter, goes to yoga once a week; it's her only opportunity to fully focus on herself. For Justine, 29, of San Diego, California, it's a Pilates exercise class that centers her—and taking her dog for a walk. Simone, 28, of San Francisco, California, finds her mental space with her workout buddies. She has a running partner and goes running three or four times a week. She finds the combination of exercise and socializing fully rejuvenates her sense of being. Other venues for finding mental space abound: book clubs; art classes; even knitting groups, such as Stitch 'n' Bitch, which are becoming quite hip in urban zones, are popular choices.

girlfriends

For a marriage to work well, it is critical that each spouse find companionship and happiness *outside* of their relationship. If you don't, you will be placing a tall order on your spouse for personal fulfillment, entertainment, and stimulation. To complicate the issue, you and your spouse may have different appetites for a social life; one of you may want two or more ventures out with friends each week, while the other wants to dedicate any spare time to the relationship. As mentioned in the last chapter, negotiating time together may be one of your biggest struggles during the first year as you begin to work out the kinks of merging two separate lives. The thing to keep in mind is not to neglect your own personal social life. Women need women friends. We are a sharing, communicating, supportive gender, and most of our husbands can't possibly provide us with the amount of stimulation we need to feel like active, spiritual members of our community. I'll talk more about nurturing friendships later on. For now, the important thing to remember is this: Keeping in touch with your friends is really about keeping in touch with yourself. So if you don't want to "lose" yourself in marriage, you must not lose your girlfriends.

boundaries

The last area you need to pay special attention to as you confront your evolving wife identity is your sense of boundaries. By boundaries I mean that sense of where you (and your desires and opinions and moods) begin and end, as opposed to those of your husband. I've found in the four years of cohabitation with my husband and in candid discussion with many other women that it's very easy for our gender to take our partner's moods personally.

It's particularly difficult, for me at least, to let my husband be in a bad mood without taking it personally or trying to "fix" the situation. When he's in a funk, I usually get anxious, especially if he doesn't want to talk about whatever's pissing him off—something at work or something that broke around the house that he's having trouble fixing. Then I get upset and feel that he's shutting me out.

During these times I try to remember boundaries. I focus on whatever I was doing before, allowing my husband the time and space he needs to work through his issues. At times I literally have to tell myself: "This is *his* mood, not mine." Once I remind myself of the mental boundary between us, I can carry on with my own business until my husband is ready to reconnect. When I try to open up that boundary before he's ready to share, it usually leads to an unsatisfying interaction between us, putting both of us into a foul temper. Boundaries are critical for maintaining a sense of individuality in marriage, especially since everything else is being merged.

FIVE

Sex for as long as you both shall live

There are two liberating aspects of married sex. One, if you and your husband get lax in the birth control department (a common phenomenon based on my admittedly unscientific observations), the possibility of conception isn't nearly as daunting as when you were single. Two, sex is always available to you (well, sort of). The funny thing is, many wedded women are relatively silent about the perks of married sex. They often change the subject when the topic of sex enters the conversation among girlfriends. Rarely do they go into graphic detail, which they may have done before marriage. Married women typically don't like to discuss their sex lives.

Before I accepted the challenge of writing a book about the first year of marriage, I worked as a producer at a women's Web site. My business card boldly listed my title as "Sex & Romance Producer." During my tenure as sex producer, I wrote a "Sexpert" column and edited articles on foreplay, orgasms, and oral sex. Then I was laid off during the dot-com bust of 2001. No matter. My writing career had already taken a new turn. I had been asked to write a sex column for the *San Francisco Chronicle*. In this column, called "About Sex," I explored myriad sex-related issues, from faulty libidos to infidelity, that single and married men and women face. This unanticipated turn toward all things sexual in my career, along with my research for this book, has given me insight into the bedrooms of hundreds of married women. In this chapter I will share with you everything I've come to know about the way your sex life may change during year one of marriage.

the positive aspects

perk #1: a surge of sensuality

Many of the women I spoke with during my interviews for this book said that their sexual energy soared during their engagement and throughout the year following their wedding. According to them, this sensual surge ultimately led to either more sex or more satisfying sex (or, in many cases as you might guess, both).

These women attributed the surge to the commitment of love and monogamy they had made with their mate. The commitment, they said, added an additional layer of optimism and trust to their relationship (and optimism and trust are the top two mental aphrodisiacs for good sex—verve to the vagina, so to speak). Other interviewees said that they simply felt sexier, having made their debut into the social club of Unobtainable Married Women. Perhaps the surge also comes from that place way back in a girl's head (or is it the heart?) of knowing that she has been chosen by her husband to share his bed with him every single night for the rest of their lives. Romantic, eh?

Some women I interviewed pointed to the spiritual aspects of sex after marriage, explaining that making the "till death do we part" vow to their lover and future father of their children gave their sex life more reverence and meaning. This is particularly true if you believe, as I do, that lovemaking is an expression of your spirituality. Some women even described the feeling as a sexual awakening. The spiritual-sexual phenomenon may also occur if your particular brand of religion made you feel guilty all those times you were engaging in sexual trysts with your lover before you exchanged your official "I do's." For you religious folk, the freedom from guilt could be the rebel yell that awakens your sensuality.

If you read the last chapter carefully, you'll recall my fantasy about becoming a housewife—baking bread and growing wild herbs for my husband and our home. While the fantasy of turning domestic first gave me panic attacks at night—I adore my writing career!—I've since realized that this fantasy has more to do with a buried longing for a more sensual life, one that ticks to human biorhythms (not an alarm clock) and is tightly wound to such sensual acts as working the earth, preparing food, and using the wind to dry my clothes. (In my fantasy I also look like Audrey Hepburn, but that's another issue, isn't it?) For me, marriage awoke that sensual part of my nature which during the year leading up to our wedding was suffocating in event planning.

The problem is, our lives are increasingly void of sensuality. We work in sterile environments with unnatural lighting and scary coworkers. Our only interaction with nature is (maybe) walking to lunch or sitting out in the sun during a five-minute coffee break. It's my suspicion that the lack of sensuality in our daily groove becomes more apparent to us after marriage, a life-altering experience during which many of us are reintroduced to the concept of "there's more to life than work"—especially soulless work. The ceremony of marriage, filled with burning candles, fragrant bouquets, soulful music, and sacred readings, invokes the senses of sound, smell, and sight unlike any other ceremony in our culture, and it takes us one step closer to our sensual and spiritual worlds. And that is a boon to our sex lives.

perk #2: a cuddly hubby

Sophie, 27, of Dallas, Texas, and her husband occasionally slip into the tub with a bottle of wine. Sex is not necessarily on the agenda (if it happens, it happens, she's quick to point out). For them the water and wine enhance the sharing of an intimate moment in which there is no pressure to perform or please one another. The goal is to indulge in the sensuality of the moment.

This is a perfect example of another post-wedding sex-related phenomenon discovered by many brides not long after their bouquets have dried: a rise in affection and tenderness. If you are lucky enough to experience this perk, your intimate moments with your mate may begin to include more cuddling, snuggling, and back-rubbing. What's more, your *mate* may be the one who initiates these tender acts of affection. According to my anecdotal research, many married men become increasingly sentimental upon tying the knot.

Now some of you cynics out there may wonder if I'm sugarcoating the real issue here: A rise in nonsexual intimacy means a decrease in wild, crazy gorilla sex, which you and your mate were relishing during your early dating years. Let's not confuse the two phenomena (although there may be a connection, I admit).

It's possible that during your former courtship days, nonsexual intimacy was simply overwhelmed by sex hormones, and now that those hormones have chilled out, as they do, other displays of intimacy are finally getting their day in the sun. At any rate, we'll address the dwindling libido issue when we get to the bummer aspects of married sex. Since I consider cozying up with your partner just as critical to sustaining a sexy love life as intercourse (that's such an unromantic word!), the increased cuddling component will remain a perk in my book.

perk #3: no more inhibitions!

A lot of ink has been devoted to the suppressed sexuality of wives across America. Frankly, I don't buy it. In fact, I've found the opposite to be true: More and more women are finding that marriage has bolstered their sexual prowess and given them the security and confidence they need to experiment more between the sheets. Maybe the reason this post-wedding sexual renaissance hasn't yet been thoroughly examined by academics is that the phenomenon is too new—as recent, perhaps, as *Sex and the City*. I don't know. But my interviews indicate that there's an impressive contingency of women who become bolder in bed after tying the knot.

Part of this phenomenon is clearly related to the security and everlastingness that marriage promises a relationship. There's nothing like having a man confess his lifelong desire to make love to you to give a girl confidence in her sexuality. The freeing sensation may also be attributed to the fact that the longer you are with the same partner, the more attuned you are to each other's bodies. Experience teaches you both which sexual techniques hit the right spots and which ones don't even come close, liberating you from sexual doubt and any fears of inadequacy you may harbor from your teenage years.

Many of you may also find that you are becoming more and more comfortable with your body. You may discover, for instance, that your husband really can't tell the difference in the circumference of your thighs when you're PMS-ing (or at least has learned the cardinal rule of being a good husband: Never tell your wife that she looks bloated). Besides, he's too busy telling you how sexy you are, right? Anyhow, body confidence does wonders for the libido.

You may also find yourself less embarrassed about such carnal evidence of mortality as vaginal farts or even the other kind. (Case in point: I *never* would have written about vaginal farts—unless in a very private email to my most discreet girlfriend—before marriage.) The more sex you have with the same partner, the more comfortable you will feel about your body, as well as giving and receiving pleasure. If that's not a bonus to marital sex, then I don't know what is.

perk #4: a happy vagina

I've saved the best perk for last. Contrary to Hollywood myth, married sex is the most satisfying sex a girl can get. It's familiar, it's emotional, it has experience, it has depth and a sense of humor, it's safe, and it has many faces: It's trampy when it wants to be, serene when desired, and, at a minimum, a good stress reliever when your mind is wrangling with your most recent credit card statement. Married sex also has a future, so it comes with built-in security and trust. Remember what I said before: Trust is the mind's greatest aphrodisiac.

Because of these attitudes, sex with your life partner, who gets constant hands-on training and frequent practice (schedules permitting) in learning how to please you, is far more satisfying than sex with a part-time lover who hasn't had the experience or incentive to memorize your nineteen erogenous zones. The only thing married sex may lack compared to unmarried sex is the obvious: the potential for variety in partners (unless, of course, you're one of those polyamorous couples).

Call me old-fashioned, but variety is overrated. Making love to the man who really knows every nuance of your body and psyche and who cares about you more than anyone else in the world (pardon the sap, but I'm trying to make a point) far outweighs a change of scenery. Bunking the myth, married sex is not tedious or rote or lacking in any way. It has its good and bad days, of course, but most of the time, when married couples complain about nonexistent sex lives, the problem lies in their overscheduled lifestyles and/or their priorities, not their sexual connection or drive.

There's one last (but definitely not least) thing I want to say about pleasure. If you are one of the many women out there whose mate has never learned which bells to jingle, or if you don't know where your bells are located or how to make them ring, you must take a refresher course on becoming orgasmic. Good Vibrations (www.goodvibes.com) is a clearinghouse of information dedicated to sexual pleasure. It can direct you to the myriad how-to reading materials and videos available for teaching women to feel pleasure.

Once you have the basic concept down on your own, it's up to you to show your partner your personal road map to orgasm. You owe this to yourself and to your marriage, which needs a satisfying sex life to carry it through the potholes and dirty laundry that all soul mates encounter along the road of life.

Now that I've mentioned potholes, it's my obligation to reveal some of the downers of married sex that many couples face during the first year's adjustment to marriage. As with any adjustment, it helps to know what to expect. Thankfully, there are only four potential bummers, and I have seven strategies for combating them in the section that follows, so there's no need to get freaked out. I'll give them to you straight.

potential downers

bummer #1: he's no longer "the lover"

He's also your roommate, your cook (sometimes), your nurse (occasionally), and your financial confidant. There are two sides to this coin, of course. You, too, are no longer your husband's night nymph. You are his therapist (daily), his social coordinator (frequently), his janitor (likely).

"In marriage you don't have the luxury of just being 'the lover,'" says marriage counselor and sex therapist Wendy Maltz, coauthor of *Private Thoughts: Exploring the Power of Women's Sexual Fantasies.* "You have to deal with the demands of running a household, so there's no separation between passion and daily living. Many of the roles you play in marriage are counter to the development of eroticism. If your partner gets the flu, for instance, you're going to get a different sense of him." Likewise, he will get a different sense of you when you're delirious and irritable with fever or just regular old exhaustion.

In other words, you may no longer be a perpetual sex kitten in your husband's mind, as you were when you were dating. He may have failed to witness, for example, the remnants of your shaving in the bathtub. We could go into the exhaustive madonna/whore complex discussion right now, which basically suggests that some men may view women as either saints or sluts and put their wives into the saint category, thereby stamping out any lustful associations they may have had for them. But I'm not too big on Freudian analysis, so I'll skip further mention. Besides, I think most modern men are more sexually enlightened than this way of thinking. I will mention, however, that your husband's growing awareness of the many roles you play as wife may affect your love life: It makes it harder for him to view you as the seductive lover who once wore matching bra and panty sets during each sexual encounter.

The *lover* persona becomes more difficult for couples to achieve primarily because they are around each other 24/7, from the disheveled moment they wake up in the morning to the baggy-eyed moment they pass out in bed at the end of the day. Not only does it take time and energy to evoke the lover mystique (by shaving your legs and possibly splashing on some seductive scent, donning sexy clothing, and even sprucing up the bedroom with candles and the like), but it also requires distance, which is one thing most couples do not have in marriage.

bummer #2: sizzle turns to simmer

I wrote above, in the "perks" part, that familiarity with your lover leads to greater pleasure, and I stand firmly by my statement. But it's my duty to warn you that familiarity also has a way of dimming the flames of passion, which are primarily fueled by mystery, anticipation, and surprise. Clearly, passion and pleasure are connected, but they are not necessarily dependent on each other. That's important to keep in mind when it comes to your sex life, because blinding passion may not play as dominant a role in your married love life.

Some sex therapists point to physiological explanations in an effort to explain why sexual desire may wane in marriage, but I'd rather not get all technical about fluctuating oxytocin levels and the libido-dampening effects of stress, physical exhaustion, and unresolved childhood issues. I'll save that for the therapists. I'd rather just make the following observation: Sexual desire waxes and wanes throughout life, regardless of whether you are in a monogamous relationship or not. Marriage breeds new relationship stresses that unmarried couples don't have to deal with. And, as I mentioned above, stress is a huge contributor to the simmering phenomenon.

While those insatiable libidos of our teenage pasts do make cameo appearances when we fall in love, almost any *honest* married woman (or, for that matter, any woman who has been monogamous for six months or longer) will admit that those all-night-long sexual longings and erotic impulses that once enabled you and your lover to make love for hours without a second thought about missing the latest *Friends* rerun are but a sweet memory from your dating days. Don't get me wrong; the sizzle is still there (most of us get back in touch with it when we're on vacation or are treated to an exceptional round of foreplay). The important thing to remember is not to get freaked out when your libido is in sleep mode.

bummer #3: you get less of it

Combine the two aforementioned bummers with the general exhaustion many married couples feel after a day of labor followed by the occasional heated discussion on finances, relatives, and whose turn it is to clean the toilet, and you may discover that, over time, you're having less sex with your husband than you used to. (Note: The added degree of cuddling, mentioned earlier as a perk, may serve as a substitute for sex, which makes this reality less harsh on

the brain.) Those of you who lived with your mate before
tying the knot will most likely not notice a decline in frequency because you already went through this adjustment
when you first moved in together. What's more, the surge,
also mentioned earlier as a perk, may produce the opposite
effect on your sex life, neutralizing this point entirely.

If you're getting it on less often, however, do not get
distressed. Shifting from making love four times a week to
once in a blue moon is a normal response to cohabitation.
(The blue moon—whatever that means—is an exaggera-
tion, by the way. According to my interviews, the norm is
once a week. Once every couple of weeks isn't so far off,
either.) Yet the decrease in sex is one of the hardest things
for many newlyweds to come to grips with, especially if
your own mom is telling you that you're not getting
enough, as is the case with one woman I interviewed. Many
of us wrongly believe that something is amiss in our sex lives
if we are not as active as we used to be.

By the way, this might be a good opportunity to mention the cardinal rule of married sex: Never compare your
sex life to that of another couple, especially your parents!
Every couple's sex style moves to a unique groove, and there
is no magic number indicating normal frequency. If you
recall, I mentioned earlier on in this chapter that married
women rarely gossip about their own sex lives. It's my theory that this is because they've learned that measuring their
sex lives against those of their friends only breeds insecurities—since most people exaggerate their sex lives and usually only mention the great aspects of it, which could cause
a girl to feel inferior about her own. Or they lie about their
amorous encounters completely. There's also that newly
developed guilt about sharing private exchanges between
you and your husband with parties outside the marital bond,

but that's really another issue. The point I want to make is this: As long as you and your husband are satisfied with your sex life, there is no problem.

bummer #4: you want it, he doesn't (or vice versa)

Those of you who cohabitated with your mate before getting hitched already know that you and your husband will not always want sex at the same time. You may already have made peace with the reality that you and your mate have very different sex drives to begin with. It's easier to mask the discrepancy in libidos when you're dating because sex is more predictable when it's available only on certain nights. You pretty much know you're going to get some whenever you get together and can therefore anticipate accordingly. Once sex becomes available every day, as when you move in together for the first time, the discrepancy often begins to reveal itself.

Alicia, 34, of Kailua, Hawaii, panicked when she first began to notice the difference in libido between her and her husband (her sex drive is stronger). "I worried about what I was going to do for the rest of my life," she recalls. "I kept thinking, 'I've missed his prime!'" (She has since figured out some tactics for navigating these differences; I'll attempt to reveal them in the next section, so sit tight.)

One of the hardest parts of having a sex drive that is different from your husband's is dealing with the rejection that goes with this dilemma. If you're the one with the stronger drive, your ego will become bruised if your mate continuously turns down your advances. You will also feel sexually frustrated. Almost as disconcerting (but not quite) is when you are the one whose libido is less active, and you must constantly turn down the advances of your husband.

This becomes exceptionally tiresome during those times when you're curled up beneath cozy covers and on the verge of falling into a delicious sleep, only to be drawn back into the harsh reality of life by an unquestionably intentional poke in the rump from your suddenly aroused husband (an act that one woman and her girlfriends have affectionately termed "binking").

Binking aside, many of you will be guaranteed a fantastic sex life during the first year of marriage simply because you are entering matrimony, which is inherently sexy by nature. If you are one of these couples (and I hope you are), I strongly advise that you keep reading the rest of this chapter anyway, because much of what I'm going to suggest is foundation for a sexy *future*. In all my research on sex, lovemaking becomes a more prickly issue between spouses later in life when kids and other stresses, such as ailing parents and an increasingly demanding work schedule, have more of an exhaustive, if not depletive, effect on the libido.

What follows is a guide to keeping your sex life full of vigor as you begin to navigate the above-mentioned sex bummers during year one.

seven-step guide to the good (sex) life

step #1: prioritize your libido

During the first year of marriage your entire lifestyle is in flux. You and your mate will be adjusting to each other's way of living and the various additional stresses that matrimony brings to the plate. Since your daily rhythms are in flux anyway, marriage offers a natural opportunity to customize your lifestyle so that sex on a frequent basis becomes a priority. Without this conscious commitment to sex—say, once or twice a week every week, no matter what—you're likely to find yourself more and more entrenched in the afore-mentioned Bummer #3 (you get less of it). Without a delib-erate commitment to your sex life, exhaustion may continu-ally override your and your spouse's libidos, and the level of sexual intimacy within your relationship drops. Sex be-comes an extra, even (dare I say) a chore. In the end these attitudes can build a wall of dissatisfaction and resentment between you and your mate.

Reinventing your lifestyle, as it relates to sex, is not a taxing endeavor. It's just a matter of openly discussing fre-quency and timing with your mate, and making sure you have plenty of opportunities to make love before you both pass out at the end of the day or dash off to work in the morning. Simone, 28, of San Francisco, California, and her husband make it a habit to hop into bed early—9 P.M., which gives them plenty of time to have sex if they find themselves in the mood.

Since exhaustion is the number one libido killer in an otherwise sexy relationship, you might also consider rein-venting the part of your lifestyle that is making you so exhausted in the first place. Are you eating energizing foods or junk? Are you exercising three to five times a week, com-bining at least thirty minutes of cardio with weight training and stretching? Are you drinking plenty of water—enough to combat all that dehydrating coffee you've been downing since morning? Are you planning enough chill time for yourself now that you're sharing your abode with another human being who is always around? Are you stretching your social calendar a little too thin to accommodate all your friends and colleagues? If so, your sex life will be com-promised.

Those of you who are overtaxed by work and social

demands might even consider scheduling sex with your partner. (I can see that grimace, but hear me out.) I recently had the opportunity to interview sex diva Laura Corn, best-selling author of *101 Nights of Grrreat Sex* and, her latest, *The Great American Sex Diet*, for one of my sex columns. According to her research, couples who schedule sex regularly—she recommends three to four times a week—have more satisfying love lives. "Some people reject the idea of scheduling sex because it's not spontaneous, no fun," Corn says. "But what they're really rejecting is having to make a commitment. People avoid intimacy because they think they have no time. Scheduling sex shows you that you do have time."

step #2: find your new groove

If the previous message hasn't sunk in yet, let me spell it out for you: Marriage changes your groove. The single girl within may spend a good portion of the first year of matrimony trying to reinvent herself in her new status of wife. She will also come to terms with what it means to no longer be a practicing member of the Eligible Babes Club. As a result, she may begin to question her sex appeal, a phenomenon briefly mentioned in the last chapter.

Adding to the dilemma is the fact that during this first year a girl often finds herself lacking downtime as she and her husband work out the kinks of cohabitation. What this means in terms of groove is that you may find yourself having less and less time to do all the girly things you used to do when you were prepping and primping for your mate: blow-dry your hair (even in the back), pluck your brows, and even choose a set of matching lingerie to surprise your lover in bed.

Before I go on, let's get one thing straight: I'm not suggesting that you exhaust yourself in an effort to look sexy for your mate (although I'm sure he wouldn't complain if that was my message; guys—husbands and bachelors alike—like surprises and variety, just as you do). I am suggesting, though, that you devote some time every day to your sensuality. You may channel your Eros by meditating while looking out the window and listening to all the night creatures begin their rounds. Or by reading erotica in a tub filled with bergamot oil. Or even by doing your P.M. Yoga tape after a sweaty workout at the gym. Regardless of your method, the point is to relax and allow yourself the opportunity to get in touch with the sensual world around you, the world composed of touch, smell, taste, and sound.

Taking full responsibility for your own sensuality is critical for a sexy marriage. True, you can conjure up arousal through interactions with your husband (such as when he tells you how beautiful the curve of your hips are in the moonlight). But since your mate is only human and can't possibly satisfy all your sensory needs, it's up to you to cultivate your own sense of arousal so the burden of sexual esteem isn't resting entirely on your mate's shoulders. Doing so will help you revitalize your groove.

step #3: throw your mate for a loop

If you find your sex life becoming a tad too predictable for your taste (as all married couples do now and then), it's up to you to do your part in adding new tension to your love life. Tension will not only help jump-start a flagging libido, but it also can make your orgasms more exciting and satisfying. Going back to the notion of how living with your lover affects your love life, once the potential for sex becomes an everyday event, some of that sexual anticipation and desire and tension loses its buildup. Without sexual anticipation you might not be getting the full bang for your buck (pardon the weird analogy, but you get the point).

One of the best ways to rebuild tension is by adding variety to your usual sexual routine. Variety isn't just about exploring new sex positions (although that helps). And variety is not solely about experimenting with sex toys, fantasies, times of day, locations, and props (although those can add zest to your sex life, too). Variety is primarily about surprising each other, so both you and your partner feel as though your sexual relationship is constantly evolving (or at least open to the idea of evolution). Challenging your sex life takes intimacy to a new level.

Erin, 27, of San Francisco, California, noticed that since she and her husband tied the knot, she has run the risk of making her sex life too formal, getting into certain patterns and shying away from things that sound "too silly" for postnuptial nooky. Something shifted in her relationship with her husband after they got married, making them feel as if they had to be more responsible when it came to making love. To combat this shift, they make a point of throwing each other for a loop. If guests are coming over in half an hour and they suddenly get horny, they make sure to appease their libidos, as they would have before marriage, instead of doing the "responsible" thing: prep for their guests so they don't answer the door with an afterglow, disheveled clothing, and an unpacked bag of groceries spilling across the kitchen floor.

The fear of getting caught is, by the way, a good tactic for stirring the embers of what might otherwise be a typical roll in the sack. Avery, 33, of New York, New York, recalls her most memorable sex experience with her husband: "We were on the balcony of our hotel room in the Bahamas about six months after we got married. We started kissing, and one thing led to another; the next thing I knew, our clothes were coming off. What made that so memorable was the fact that we were outside, and it felt sort of taboo. Someone could have seen us."

step #4: practice the art of initiation

In any long-term monogamous relationship, it's critical for both partners to do an equal share of initiating sex. If the initiation becomes one-sided—your husband rolls on top of you every night and begins a full-throttled body rub, hoping it'll arouse you, to use a stereotypical example—the balance of power in your relationship runs the risk of getting out of whack, especially if you (again, forgive the stereotype) are constantly rejecting your husband's advances. But more on that in a minute. Matching your husband's initiation efforts will make your mate feel attractive and loved and wanted, and that will help keep your sexual intimacy fully engaged.

Initiation, by the way, is an art. It requires a delicate mix of seduction, boldness, and vulnerability (you are risking rejection, you know, and even with a partner of many years, it still sucks when you try out a suggestive move and your husband tells you he's not in the mood). Amber, 30, of San Francisco, California, is as bold as a bee when it comes to initiation. There have been moments, she says, when she really needs sexual release. "I'll take my husband's hand and simply lead him into the bedroom and tell him, 'We need to do this now.'" Mindy, 25, of Somerset, New Jersey, takes the playful approach when she initiates. "Sometimes I'll start fighting over the covers. That turns into giggling, which then leads to sex."

step #5: offer an alternative

Since every sexually active woman will experience times in marriage when she's not in the mood, getting her period and experiencing body-curling cramps, or is otherwise too exhausted for sex, there will be other times when she must turn down her partner's attempts at seduction. This is to be expected in a long-term monogamous relationship. But there are gentle and tame ways to turn down your lover. The best approach to rejection, say sex therapists, is to first reiterate how much you love and desire your partner. Then mention how your momentary dip in libido has nothing to do with his gorgeous hunk of masculinity but, rather, your (fill in the blank—period/stomachache/horrible day at work).

If you're feeling exceptionally generous (given your state of exhaustion or whatever), offer your husband an alternative, such as a foot massage. Or suggest opening a bottle of wine or building a fire together and lying down in front of it fully clothed rather than getting naked and phys-ical. Or consider one of the greatest alternative suggestions I've come across: When Barbara, 30, of Staten Island, New York, is too tired for sex, she agrees to have it—but only on the condition that her husband does all the work. Usually, she admits, once they get started, her adrenaline turns on, and she ends up getting into it and participating. But having the license to do nothing but lie there and receive the plea-sure, if she chooses, helps get her going. (Warning: Upon hearing this technique, I decided to try it out on my hus-band. When I suggested he do all the work, he laughed in my face. Now he says it to me! But who knows, it may work for you.)

One caveat about rejecting your partner: Don't make it

a habit. As you probably know, rejection stings, especially if the rebuff is coming from the one person to whom you're most willing to bare your body and soul. When you reject lovemaking, you're ultimately rejecting intimacy. "Sexual intimacy takes physical energy and emotional energy, so it requires more effort than, say, going to the gym," says Corn. "We have to let go of emotional layers that push us away from our partners. When we make love, we're letting go of those emotional blocks. It's healing." Corn points out that it often takes more energy to reject your partner (coming up with excuses, feeling guilty, and then dealing with the fights that ensue over how often you make love, for instance) than it does to actually make love. Just something to consider.

step #6: take a trip

Each year reserve at least two vacations (one of which is at least one week long) to be spent solely with your partner. These trips must not include friends or family. Why the mandatory isolation and time requirements? You need these breaks from reality to dissociate from your daily routines and to relax so you can enjoy the romance that's inherent in traveling to a place where climate and food are equally exotic. Besides, there is nothing like a vacation to remind you and your lover how sexy the other one is. Part of that magic has to do with removing yourselves from the backdrop of daily life, where you continuously butt heads with the lover-roommate conundrum.

Vacation sex is typically some of the best sex you'll have with your husband, because so much of the stress that holds us back during our day-to-day has been lifted. The change of scenery also serves to bring a little fantasy into the bedroom; when you're staying at a cheap hotel, you can fantasize that you're having a tawdry affair with your husband, for instance. Or if you're at a lodge in Tahoe, you can pretend you're both back in college and horny as hell. If your vacations are typically nature-oriented, then you get to experience the rawness and liberation of making love under a warm sun, in a warm wind, or, if you're feeling particularly free, in warm water—elemental sexual acts that are hard to come by in urban (suburban) living.

step #7: immediately hand this book to your husband

Guys, I'm here to let you in on a little secret for the betterment of your monogamous lifestyle. Your wife needs *more foreplay.* Here's how it works (I'll use a sports analogy for simplicity's sake): In order to get into the game, our female physiques require a very, very long warmup. The warmup is needed not only to relax our muscles, but also to get us mentally prepared for the main event.

A really good warmup will begin by engaging our minds, since strategizing and visualizing are critical to playing a good game. More specifically, most of us would like **advance notice** that you are in the mood so we can psych ourselves up for the game. That means hints in the morning and suggestive emails throughout the day, indicating what you have in mind for the evening. Next, the warmup should **engage critical muscles** (and surrounding area) necessary for action. Precisely, this means at least fifteen to twenty minutes of kissing—starting with the lips and then slowly making your way downward. Hearing repeated **intoxicating affirmations** such as "You are so incredibly sexy!" or similar are also welcome. Don't worry if they sound clichéd. Any basic sex-appeal affirmation will do.

A girl needs said warmup *every* time you wish to make love to her. Occasionally she will try to skip the warmup and may even balk at the very notion, so eager is she to engage in a little one-on-one (a.k.a. "the quickie"). But typically, when she skips the warmup, her ability to engage with full enthusiasm and spirit will be compromised. Therefore, always insist on foreplay. The longer the two of you can stretch out the warmup, the better the game will be.

Not long after Lawrence and I got engaged, we went to see a stand-up comedian by the name of Mike Dugan at The Marsh theater in San Francisco. His show was called "Men Fake Foreplay," a concept that truly horrified me at the time. Do men fake foreplay? I kept waiting for the critical punch line (it *had* to be a joke, right?), but his show was cut short by Robin Williams, who leapt out of the audience and onto the stage, and then burst into a two-hour nonstop improvisation on everything from the Last Supper to hands-free cell phone usage in the streets of San Francisco.

I'm a fan of Robin Williams and all, but, frankly, I wanted more foreplay (as does your wife, I'll risk repeating). Do men fake foreplay? (Lawrence, suspiciously, had no comment.) The answer, I found out later after frantically scanning promotional materials from Dugan's show, was, frighteningly, yes. Men fake their enthusiasm for foreplay, Dugan suggests, because women fake orgasms. Yikes! This madness must stop!

Which leads me to my last point about foreplay: What your wife really wants is honest, open discussion on what each of you likes and doesn't like between the sheets. Communication is just as much a part of foreplay as groping and panting. Exploring each other's sensuality as it exists in your fantasies might not hurt, either, because open talk about the most intimate part of your life together usually leads to an emotional closeness and vulnerability that, quite frankly, serves as the foundation for any great sexual relationship. Especially one that has to last a lifetime.

$\mathcal{M}$oney

Ick.

That's the first word that comes to mind when I think about money and marriage. The two are just so unromantic when you put them together! Ask any newly married woman what she and her husband argue about most, and she'll likely answer—without a moment's pause, I might add—money. (She'll also mention the in-laws and division-of-labor wars, but money usually tends to fly right out of her mouth without too much thought.)

To make matters worse, statisticians claim that the number one cause of divorce is conflict over money. Before I got married, that stat always perplexed me. How could *money* cause divorce? Now, in my wizened state of matrimony, I understand the connection. Clearly, money *itself* isn't the source of our nation's unprecedented divorce rate, which these days hovers around 50 percent (although you have got to wonder about that when you look at how closely the rise in divorce parallels the rise in women's earning power). Socioeconomics aside, I would argue that not being able to negotiate differences in managing, making, spending, and saving money is ultimately the underlying evil.

What makes the money negotiations so difficult compared to, say, the dividing-up-chores negotiations or the spending-time-with-mother-in-law negotiations or even the it's-your-turn-to-initiate-sex negotiations is the fact that our futures (in terms of feeling financially secure and being able to realize all our dreams) are disproportionately dependent upon money. And most things in life that have a direct impact on our future provoke a disproportionate amount of fear, passionate insistence, and the need to control—traits that greatly interfere with successful negotiation.

The other reason money disagreements are so much more passionate than other differences between spouses is that our autonomy is intricately linked to money's power. As married women we are no longer solely responsible for paying household debts and determining what takes priority in our life, such as setting up an emergency savings account or going to Cabo for a two-week vacation. We have to confer with our partner on the big financial decisions. What's more, most of us enter marriage with work experience and a self-supporting salary that in many cases competes, if not outshines, that of our husband. No longer is our gender entering the state of matrimony with economic dependence and/or ignorance, and that dynamic often leads to power struggles.

Learning how to share the responsibility of managing the marital finances can at times feel constricting, as though you've lost your independence and your control over your future. The truth is that in marriage you *are* letting go of your autonomy, and any resistance you may have to that release is frequently played out in financial discussions. To put it bluntly, it's fairly easy to fake a happy marriage until you begin the process of merging assets. Money has a way of provoking conflict.

I hope I haven't scared you too much, but I'm just trying to give you an accurate picture of the reality of money's presence in marriage. As you read through this chapter, which is filled with advice from those of us who've been through the process of merging finances with our mates, keep the following in mind: Sharing financial responsibility with your spouse is a process that will always be evolving. The hardest part about it will likely hit you during the first year of marriage when you design a system that works for both of you (and then redesign it a few months later when you discover its flaws). The second hardest part about sharing money will be getting used to living within the new financial structure you and your mate design because both of you will likely be dealing with money differently from what you are used to.

bookkeeping for two

For simplicity's sake, let's break down the entire subject of money and marriage into two categories: management and philosophy. The easier category to deal with when you're entering the business of marriage (remember that analogy from Chapter 3) is money management because there are concrete rules you and your husband can set without expending too much emotional energy (at least in theory). The category of money philosophy is far more amorphous and emotional, but we'll get to that beast in a bit. For now, let's stick to basic bookkeeping.

Within the arena of money management, there are three basic parts that all couples need to get a grip on at some point during the first year of marriage: debt, spending, and savings. Let's dissect each of these.

debt

Most of us entering marriage will have some degree of debt weighing us down: the bar tab from the wedding where all of our friends got trashed (in a celebratory way, of course), lingering student loans, that frightful Macy's card which we used to charge all of our fancy makeup products for the wedding day, and the VISA card that sponsored our entire honeymoon. Unless you received a bounty of cash from generous wedding guests to pay off some of these debts, you will need to come up with an aggressive plan for getting rid of it soon after you tie the knot. If you've ever read anything about personal finance, you already know that debt is a plague on your financial health. If you don't attack debt swiftly and vigorously with the antibiotic of an aggressive payback plan, it will begin to consume your marital well-being because debt prevents you and your husband from moving forward and feeling optimistic. During the first year of marriage, all you'll really want to do is focus on the future.

Since there are so many different types of debt (student loans, credit cards, mortgage—if you've entered the territory of home ownership—car loans, and personal loans from family or friends), and since you most likely can't pay it all back at once, you and your husband must first take inventory of everything you owe. Then you must compare the interest rates on each of these loans. From there you can make a plan as to which loans to pay off first (hint: those with the highest interest rates). Also, you can consider whether or not you want to consolidate various loans, if possible; you may be able to combine all your credit card debt on one card with a low interest rate or consolidate your student loans so you have only one bill a month instead of two. This will at least help eliminate bill stress.

The discussion on how to approach your marital debt will obviously lead to wider-ranging money talks, such as whether or not you should pay off your individual debts on your own or inherit each other's debts as a symbol of your unity and pay them all off together. Muriel, 30, of Portland, Oregon, decided to take on her husband's credit card and student loan debts when they got hitched. Her husband had been in school getting a Ph.D. and she had been working, so she paid off her husband's debts so they could start off financially with a clean slate. She didn't resent doing that, she says, because the money he owed was basically due to the cost of being a student, and she felt spoiled because her parents had paid for her education. Nevertheless, inheriting her husband's debts scared her because she had never had any type of debt before. This was entirely new terrain.

The discussions on how to approach debt almost always lead to the bigger discussion on whether or not to combine incomes, thereby creating a joint account from which to pay these debts. Regardless of how you plan to pay back debt, it's important to bring all of your debt out of the closet during the first year of marriage—*especially* if you failed to discuss these things before tying the knot, as many couples do—because the amount of money each of you owes will directly affect the amount of money each of you can spend per paycheck. Your debt (and debt history) will also affect your ability to get future loans, such as a mortgage, so it's critical that you and your partner straighten out any potential problems now rather than later.

Since credit cards are often the greatest culprit when it comes to financial woe, it's also important to address their future role in your marriage—specifically, how many cards you and your mate want to have. The magic number is three. Financial planners advise both partners to keep a separate card in their own name, because it will keep each one's credit history active, which is important for getting future loans if you need them, joint or separate. I'd like to add that separate credit cards are important to have just so you and your husband have some degree of financial independence, which will help prevent that loss-of-autonomy feeling when marriage and money are mixed. That way, too, when you buy your husband a present, he won't have to know how much you spent on him. Likewise, notes Jill, 25, of Kansas City, Missouri, when your husband treats you to a bouquet of flowers, you won't have to scrutinize the bank statement to see how much he spent on you (and then worry about whether or not you have enough money to splurge on flowers). The only caveat here is trusting that you both will use these cards within your means. In other words, never buy items that you can't pay off as soon as the bill arrives (or at least within a few months in worst-case scenarios).

On that note, I also recommend that you and your husband get a third card in both your names, which you will share. Unless you have a problem with paying off debt, a joint credit card can really simplify bookkeeping. On this card you can put your Internet provider monthly fee, your newspaper subscription, gas, and other items that take a lot more time to purchase with cash. That said, it's critical that you use this card for convenience only and pay off the balance every month. That way you won't start paying interest on such inane items as toothpaste. Dara, 27, of Tampa, Florida, and her husband allow themselves a predetermined sum to charge on their joint credit card each month. And, yes, they pay that off as soon as the bill arrives.

spending

I'm not going to get into the whole spending-versus-saving philosophical debate here. I'll save that for the section on money philosophy, which we'll get to momentarily. For now, let's focus on the easier topic of managing your cash flow—that is, determining how much you and your soul mate can spend each month on joint expenses and entertainment. Since the two of you will now be sharing a home and related expenses such as groceries and cable, getting a grip on how much each of you contributes to the family fund each month is paramount to maintaining good financial health. Whether you and your husband decide on separate or joint checking accounts, you'll still need to come up with some sort of spending budget because you will not only be sharing expenses for your home, but you will also be sharing plans for your future.

To determine your budget, you must first get a grip on all your monthly expenses—the fixed ones, such as rent and utilities, as well as the variable ones, which include entertainment and groceries. To get an accurate assessment, consider tracking every penny for one week—from the cappuccino your husband purchases on his way to work, to the cost of your yoga class. Add these up and multiply by four to get an approximate month's worth. Then add that number to all your other monthly expenses, gathered from bills and your bank statement.

This will give you a rough estimate of how much you and your husband are spending each month. Once you compare that number to the money you and your mate bring into the household, you can look more closely at *how* you're spending your hard-earned cash and make adjustments accordingly. By the way, those "adjustments" are what typically cause the most tension when discussing money with your mate because they often invoke tumultuous debate on lifestyle priorities. But, again, I'm jumping ahead to the spending-versus-saving section, which we'll get to soon.

I've found that the easiest way to manage mutual spending is by opening up a joint account that is used for all your basic living costs. Most of the hitched women I interviewed have settled on this system, praising the convenience that a joint account offers. The basic premise is this: Each spouse's income goes into one pot—a joint checking and/or savings account. From this account a couple can write checks for all household bills and use their accompanying debit cards for various joint expenses, such as groceries, entertainment, dry cleaning, and sundry purchases for the home.

Within this group of couples who favor the joint approach to finances there are two subgroups: some use their joint account for personal *and* joint expenses; others prefer to keep personal money in individual checking or savings accounts, separate from the communal pot.

My husband and I began our first year of marriage by trying out this latter technique. All of our earnings went into our joint account, but a little bit of that was transferred monthly (or whenever we felt rich) into our individual checking accounts for our own private splurges on clothing, toys, trips away with friends (when the partner wasn't invited), classes, and presents for each other—however we desired.

Having separate accounts for personal spending freed us both from feeling guilty about spending money on ourselves. We also felt free because we did not have to justify our personal expenditures to each other (although neither of us scrutinized the other's spending habits, so it was a little unfounded and perhaps was based on fear). After a while, though, transferring money became tedious, and we gradually closed our personal accounts. Now all our expenses—personal and private—come from our joint account. But it took some time to get used to the idea of sharing finances with each other, and these personal accounts in the beginning helped with the transition.

Some couples, on the other hand, have completely separate accounts and divvy up bills as they come in, each handling his or her own bookkeeping. While this may be the ideal solution for those who have tried joint checking only to find that the bills never get paid and/or sharing money always made them angry at each other, I would encourage all newlyweds to at least give joint checking a shot at some point during their first year of marriage. The reason is that merging money forces you and your mate to talk about the way you spend as well as how you'd like to finance your goals for the future. Coming up with a budget for two (and then sticking to it) forces you and your husband to work as a team, negotiating your priorities and principles in ways that will help you down the road when bigger issues that require even more elaborate teamwork arise.

One of the reasons some couples shun the idea of joint checking is that one partner is anal about bookkeeping (recording checks, debit charges, and ATM withdrawals in the checkbook ledger and then religiously reconciling the balance with the monthly bank statement), while the other withdraws from the bank with abandon, leaving no record as to how the balance dropped $500 in a few days. Leigh, 29, of Orlando, Florida, didn't realize how differently she and her husband spent money until she got their first bank statement. Her husband hadn't kept a checkbook ledger in years, so he wasn't used to keeping track of his purchases or receipts. Whatever the ATM machine balance said was how much money he had to spend. This did not bode well with Leigh, who opened their first joint bank statement and nearly had a heart attack.

In these cases I recommend a compromise: The carefree partner promises to keep receipts and then place them in a predetermined spot at home. The conscientious partner promises to let go of the notion of balancing the checkbook to the penny and agrees to update their records once a week or so instead of daily. Merging finances is all about compromise. And trust.

One way to simplify the bookkeeping is to consider banking online or keeping track of expenses with a computer program. These alternatives give each partner complete access to the joint account at any time. You can pay your bills online (i.e., no more hunting for stamps or accruing a late payment fee because you forgot to put a payment in the mail), and you can see exactly where your money goes every single day, if you wish, instead of waiting for your monthly statement. In other words, online banking eliminates stress, and when it comes to money (and your marriage, for that matter), any type of stress you can eliminate is a noble cause. Leigh, by the way, highly recommends computerized banking; it has helped her and her husband's variant bookkeeping practices. "Putting our finances on the computer, figuring out and agreeing to a budget, and then sticking to it hasn't solved all of our problems," she says, "but it has helped tremendously."

Another newlywed issue that often pops up is the question of who will manage the bookkeeping. In our house we take turns, managing the money in three-month shifts. We do this for a few reasons. One, neither of us particularly wants the stress and added burden of managing the household finances every single month of the year. Two, we both want to keep in touch with what's going on with our money so we can talk intelligently and realistically about our future financial goals, and taking turns helps keep us attuned. And, finally, we think it's important to trust each other when it comes to managing the household funds. Since I'm a control freak, I found it particularly difficult after tying the knot to let go of all the bookkeeping responsibilities—even if only for a few months at a time. When my husband took his first shift of managing our finances, I took enormous pains not to micromanage his effort. I did anyway, but thank God that Lawrence (who is incredibly savvy when it comes to money, I should mention) is patient! In any event, I'm learning to let go of my anal tendencies when it comes to bookkeeping. And passing the buck of financial responsibility to my mate every few months teaches me to trust, which is essential for our relationship during the long haul.

savings

Every couple should think about creating three types of savings accounts during the first year of marriage (if they don't exist prior to exchanging your vows, that is): emergency savings, retirement savings, and the fantasy fund. While I'm not one to tell people how to live their lives (but I love offering suggestions, if you haven't already noticed), I would advise newlyweds to strive to get all three types of savings accounts into some sort of recognizable form by the time they uncork the champagne bottle to celebrate their first anniversary. Doing so will not only make you feel exceptionally responsible but will also help you create a system that will further simplify bookkeeping complications. Have you noticed how much I dig simplification?

The **emergency savings account** will help put you and your husband at ease in the event one of you loses your job or a similar tragedy strikes, such as a fender-bender that ends up costing you several thousand dollars. Financial advisers suggest that couples keep three to six months' worth of expenses in this account, but if you're the paranoid type, go ahead and build a nest that will cushion you and your mate for up to a year if it makes you feel better. Any money beyond a year's worth of living expenses is really better placed in an account that pays a higher interest rate.

Since many couples wipe out their savings to foot the bill for the wedding, you may need to start from scratch in opening this account. Your main objective is to establish an account in which your money is readily available when you need it. There are traditional savings accounts at banks, which are very safe and therefore yield almost no interest, and then there are money market accounts and short-term bond funds at banks and brokerage firms. They are also safe (meaning they are federally insured) but offer slightly higher interest. Place your money in one of these higher-earning accounts. Talk to your bank or brokerage firm about your options.

If you're feeling exceptionally adventuresome within the realm of conservative investments, consider putting a portion of your emergency savings—say 10 percent—in a short-term certificate of deposit, which is equally safe and yields even higher returns. That way some of your emergency money can earn even more interest than it would biding its time for a purpose within a money market account. If an emergency hits you tomorrow, chances are you won't need all your savings at once; you'll probably have some breathing room to let your CD mature (and earn you money in the process).

If you have very little savings, it may make financial sense to combine your joint checking and savings accounts into one money market fund with check-writing capabilities. Once you've built up enough cash to establish a proper savings account, consider separating the two and investing the savings as mentioned above. (Separating your emergency money from the money used to pay monthly expenses helps prevent that delusion of being rich when you're really not.)

The second type of savings account to get in order is your **retirement savings account**, most commonly known as a 401(k) plan or IRA. Most likely you and your mate have already started a retirement savings plan through work or a brokerage firm, but marriage is a good opportunity to reassess your investment plans and work out a strategy to maximize your various long-term earnings.

If you don't already have a retirement fund gathering monetary momentum, what are you waiting for? Financial advisers have been urging the masses for years to get off their asses and set one up. It seems our nation's Social Security system is staggeringly dated and increasingly ineffective, and if you and your mate want to maintain some sort of decent lifestyle once you retire, you *both* need to start setting aside 10 to 15 percent of your earnings now, and invest them in long-term growth stocks, indexes, and mutual funds. Financial adviser David Bach, author of *Smart Couples Finish Rich*, says that women, in particular, are less likely than men to max out their 401(k) offerings, but it's critical for them to do so. A husband's 401(k) plan most likely cannot fund a decent retirement for two, unless his investments were miraculous or he is very, very rich to begin with. Besides, two retirement funds are always better than one.

Not only does maxxing out your retirement fund contribution enable you to amass more money in your retirement account, but it will also reduce your taxable income. Now that you will be filing taxes under the status of married, you may need this extra reduction to help offset the so-called marriage penalty. But we'll talk more about taxes later.

You and your husband may have different investment strategies for retirement, and that's perfectly fine (and normal, I might add). According to Bach, married couples don't generally need to worry about how coordinated their disparate accounts are until they're closer to retirement and more likely to draw from those funds. Bach does urge his clients, however, to invest as aggressively as they can. In fact, he advises women to invest even more aggressively than men because a woman is statistically more likely to outlive her husband, meaning that she will need to live off her retirement fund longer than her mate. Since women still don't earn equal pay for equal work, it's even more critical to grow our money while we can, and aggressive investments are one way to do that.

Once you've maxxed out your 401(k) and/or IRA(s), you might also consider putting any extra money you want to designate for retirement or long-term goals, such as a college fund for future children, into a Roth IRA. The main benefit of a Roth IRA, as opposed to other IRAs available, is that you don't have to pay taxes on the money when you withdraw it. Unlike a 401(k) plan, however, you cannot write off your contributions to a Roth IRA. But if you're maxxing out your 401(k) offerings anyway, that shouldn't be a deterrent.

The final savings account you and your mate should consider opening during the first year of marriage is what I call the **fantasy fund**. If you're anything like me and my husband, the fantasy fund will remain exactly that—a fantasy. But if you have more cash to play with than we do, you should consider putting some money into a separate savings account for all those big-ticket items you and your husband will begin to desire after tying the knot, the most common being a house, a baby, and a dishwasher.

The benefits of having such an account is that it will help you and your husband save for your joint goals. If you keep any extra money in your checking accounts, chances are it will inexplicably *disappear* within a few months. Dinners out, spontaneously spending the night in Napa at a cute B & B instead of driving home after a day of wine tasting, and picking up an outdoor grill on a lark all add up. And then you won't have any money left over for a vacation! Setting aside a fixed sum every month in a fantasy savings account (or adding it in a lump sum whenever a river of cash unexpectedly inundates your bank account) will enable you and your husband to save for all those big-ticket items.

Since this money is meant to be saved for a particular goal, it's best to be conservative with it in terms of investing. "Always invest based on your timeline," says Bach, who advises the following strategy: "If you're planning to use this money in one to three years, invest it in money market and bond funds. If you're going to use the money in three to five years, put it away in bonds or balanced funds. And if you're not going to touch it for five or more years, invest in stock funds."

money philosophy

Throughout this chapter I've alluded to the ambiguous topic of money philosophy. I define the term as the way a person relates to money (that is, spending versus hoarding versus investing) as well as his or her personal beliefs about the importance of money in one's life.

Experts typically trace these philosophies to our up-bringing, explaining that most of us learned how to relate to

152 **julia bourland**

money from the intentional (more often unintentional) influences of our parents or various childhood occurrences that had life-alternating impacts on our worldview. But I would also argue that all of us have certain inborn traits that influence the way we relate to the universe. Money is just one aspect of modern living with which our unique biological impulses must contend. The trouble lies in the fact that everyone crawls into the marital bed with preexisting philosophies about money, and in many cases they just don't jibe.

when a spender marries a saver

Based on my research, the most common example of mismatched philosophies is when a spender ties the knot with a saver. Perhaps the simple reality of opposites attracting is what precipitates this dynamic. Or maybe it's more a matter of two lovers feeling like gluttons for punishment. Of course, it could just be an unfortunate fluke. Whatever the reason a spender finds himself hitched to a saver, the end result is probably one of the most challenging matches on Earth. The two philosophies are diametrically opposed.

Dara and her husband are a typical example. "Here's the problem," she explains. "We have different financial goals, so we have different attitudes toward money and how we should spend or save it. My husband wants to save everything we make besides our living expenses so he can retire young. His dad lost his thirty-year job when he was in high school, and that really affected him. He wants to be prepared for emergencies and never have to be concerned about finances. I also want to save and for him to retire young, but at the same time I feel that we should enjoy the money we're making now. I don't like that 'live for tomorrow' attitude."

Living with this dynamic is best dealt with by scheduling

periodic money talks with your mate ("money dates," as some financial planners euphemistically call them). In these dates a couple can discuss their divergent money philosophies, goals, and strategies. Leigh, a saver married to a spender, says she's much better at managing the household income and has taken on the responsibility for the past couple of years. She found that her husband had no clue as to how much it cost to run their household, making it harder for him to stay on track with his spending. If she sits down with him and shows him all the monthly reports of their spending versus savings, he is much better at not overindulging.

Dara, who has been working on a plan that she and her saver husband can both live with, agrees that regular discussion is key to living with different attitudes toward money. "Figuring out this money issue really takes a lot of communication and working together, plus sitting down with your bills and talking about a budget," she says. "When you do that, money isn't just an issue hanging over your heads but the means to a goal you can really work toward."

Chloe, 26, of Santa Barbara, California, who is a spender married to a saver, also believes that money talks are key to living with differences. Working on the goal of buying a house with her husband has taught her how to be more money cautious. For instance, instead of getting her hair done at a salon, her husband colors it for her at home. "I'm on an allowance of mad money that I spend only on myself," she explains. "Having that money is a relief; I don't need to worry about getting us into debt. Meanwhile, we've been able to save for a down payment. I've never had so much money in my account."

Clearly, establishing rules and limits is one way to tackle these differences. The important thing to remember is that each of you must contribute to the development of that budget. Otherwise, power struggles and resentment may creep into your dealings with money. Sometimes you and your mate may even find yourselves faced with a common sub-dynamic. Let's call it the good guy/bad guy syndrome. "I'm the bad guy," admits Allison, 27, of Dallas, Texas. "My husband and I have different spending habits. I'm all about budgeting; he's all about 'everything will work out, let's go have fun.'"

If you're a spender/saver couple, it's prudent to prepare for this dynamic by establishing clear consequences if one of you should grossly veer from the budget you drafted. In the past, Muriel has taken the hard-ass approach to her husband's spending. "For a while my husband went on a shopping spree," she recalls. "It started with an orchid he bought me, which was sweet. Then he got another one. Then another. Suddenly our sunroom was filled with orchids—we had two hundred!

"So he built himself a 12-by-20-foot greenhouse, and now he wants to start up an Internet business to pay for them. This scares the shit out of me and pisses me off because suddenly all our money is gone, and we're just accruing more debt. He has two thousand orchids now, and he spends all his free time hanging out with the grannies talking about them." When her husband's spending first started getting out of control, endearing as his new hobby may have been, Muriel sat him down and took away his debit card for a few months. Her husband agreed it was the best thing to do.

brie versus cheddar (and other lifestyle disputes)

Closely related to the spender-versus-saver marriage is the marriage in which two partners desire different types of lifestyles—for instance, one partner idealizes a minimalist approach to living, and the other lavishes in the high life. In these cases the tension that underlies the money talks does not come from disputes on how much to put away into a savings account each month but, rather, how to spend the funds that are designated for your joint monthly spending. Here's a very simplistic example: One of you wants to spend the bare minimum on food (cheddar on rye is fine for lunch) and would rather spend joint funds on updating your CD collection and giving donations to Greenpeace. Meanwhile, the other would prefer to stock the kitchen with Brie and brioche, figuring he or she can get copies of desired CDs on tape from friends and volunteer at a local Save the Whales campaign instead.

Jamie, 28, of Newport Beach, California, can relate (especially to the food analogy). The biggest fights in her marriage have been about money, particularly the differences between her and her husband's lifestyle expectations. She and her husband got into the habit of going out to eat every night for dinner but then decided to start cooking at home to save some money, which was fine with Jamie because she loves to cook. To kick off their new dining regimen, she decided to make a salad with artichoke hearts. At the grocery store she spent $200 on food, not even looking at prices. In her mind groceries are groceries, an irrefutable living expense not to be scrutinized by the budget keeper. Her husband, though, blew up because she spent $30 on artichoke hearts when the point of eating at home was to *save* money.

Molly, 31, of Philadelphia, Pennsylvania, experiences similar differences in spending styles with her husband. He likes to spend their joint funds on what she calls "his toys," expensive items, such as big-screen TVs and cars. She prefers to have less joint spending money and more personal money so she can, say, buy a $250 suit on a whim. The problem is, those big-ticket items come out of their joint funds since she and her husband benefit equally from them, leaving less money for her private stash of cash. Remember those "adjustments" I mentioned earlier in the spending section of this chapter? Well, Molly's dilemma is a perfect example of how all married couples are constantly forced to negotiate their spending styles—agreeing to spend less on clothing in lieu of a bigger TV (even if you, personally, don't want a bigger TV) and then getting your husband to give up his dream of a new Saab at least until your wardrobe meets standard approval.

As with the spender/saver marriage scenario, negotiating differences in lifestyle requires communication and willingness to compromise. When she gets bogged down in the mundane chore of budgeting, one woman I interviewed said she and her husband make a list of items they want, whether it's something for the house or a two-week vacation. Then they rate each item individually—high, low, or medium priority—and compare notes. Items that received two highs go to the top of the list, those with two lows head to the bottom. The mediums and mixed ratings are then negotiated somewhere in between, allowing each partner a chance to argue for or against those items.

As you and your mate discuss your lifestyle expectations, it's critical to talk about what each of you values in life—security, *carpe diem*, education, personal beauty (which costs money when you add all the clothing and hair products needed to achieve your aesthetic ideals), adventure, family, and the list goes on. Narrowing down your core values is one way to help you and your partner get a grip on how money can or can't contribute to the things you truly care about. Once you really understand what your values are, as opposed to what you want to buy, you can design a lifestyle that will help complement the values you both share.

For instance, if both of you discover that one of your core values is having a stable home life, it may make it easier to start saving for a down payment for a house instead of going gambling in Reno—an expenditure that lifts your spirits only momentarily if you're the gambler type. One of my core values is adventure, which I've always associated with traveling to exotic places (i.e., costly airfares). Through various discussions I've been having with my husband lately, I've begun to open up to the idea that the adventure I seek doesn't have to come from foreign travel; it can also come by way of a three-day backpacking venture along northern California's coast.

Another core value of mine is living a creative life (which costs more money than you'd think, considering that most creative jobs pay less than those designed by corporations to generate money). Living the life of a writer may not make me rich (and, due to its unpredictable nature, places more of the burden of financing our lifestyle on my husband), but it does allow me to live my life with integrity and in accordance with my values. In my own defense, though, I should also mention that I try to take on more of the daily household duties to make up for the fact that I don't have to commute every day. I might also add that I made more money than my mate did this year, so I'm not feeling too guilty about my choice of career at this point.

Now that I've opened the "who makes more money" can of worms, let's go ahead and discuss how that may or may not affect your marriage. But before we do, one last word on the lifestyle issue: I'm not promising any miracles resulting from money talks, ones that will end all conflicts you and your partner are struggling with. But I can promise that if you and your mate have conflicting philosophies toward money, they're not going to get any easier to live with if you suffer in silence. Communication, once again, is critical.

the contribution issue

Experts (and many couples) may disagree with me on this one—especially those who herald pre-nup agreements—but I'll risk professional embarrassment in my tirade: Married couples must not live tit for tat. In other words, however you decide to manage your duo income—in joint or separate accounts—you should not determine how much each of you gets to spend on yourself based on how much each of you earns. That is not being a team player!

The tit-for-tat lifestyle is typically born from a lack of trust (or a lack of compromise capabilities), so if you give into it and let it dominate your relationship, you will always have a wall between you and your mate. You're both in this marriage together, and neither career choices nor the economy (which financially rewards certain careers more than others) should ever play a role in human intimacy.

If you do live by the tit-for-tat ethos, power struggles and feelings of resentment could eventually surface. You also might be denying yourself a level of intimacy yet unimagined. Besides, what are you going to do if one of you suddenly becomes unemployed or takes time off from work to raise a baby? Or wants to go back to school to increase your future earning potential? Or start a business of your own? If you are both contributing to the family's well-being—whether that's by bringing in money or by taking over more of the household duties so the working partner can have a more relaxed life outside the office—money should not be the guiding light.

Because many of us were reared to treat money as though it was larger than life, some of us experience human emotions when we regard it, particularly when the contribution issue comes up. The most common emotions I heard throughout my interviewing (at least the negative emotions worth mentioning here) are guilt and resentment. The resentment may surface if you or your mate feels the other one isn't earning enough or isn't contributing equally to support the lifestyle you both want to live.

One woman I spoke with admits she felt resentful that her husband didn't make more money—a feeling that emerged only after she quit her job to pursue a new career path, prompting the two to live off one salary. Quick to acknowledge the unfairness of her resentment (she did quit her job, after all), the interviewee does recognize the ultimate cause of her resentment: Her husband isn't motivated by money in the same way she is. This realization has led her to the daunting reality that if she ever wants to be rich, it's up to her to make that happen. Other types of resentment may grow out of dated stereotypes and philosophies toward money, such as money (or trinkets bought with money) are indicative of how much your partner loves you. Any girl who feels resentful about the contribution issue should determine where those feelings come from and then discuss them with her partner.

As for guilt, well, the typical scenario is when one partner feels guilty for spending money on him- or herself. Jill traces this guilt to a fear of being (or appearing to be) selfish in the eyes of your partner—even if both are contributing equally to the marital loot. Kathleen, 27, of Portland, Oregon, recalls one particular incident in which she felt money guilt. "My husband and I went shopping for an anniversary present. I wanted earrings until the saleswoman pulled out this gorgeous bracelet, which I then immediately wanted but I thought it cost too much. My husband urged me to get both the earrings and the bracelet, but I couldn't do it. We got the earrings and left the store. In the parking lot my husband could tell how sad I was, so we ran back into the store and got the bracelet after all."

If guilt enters your spectrum of emotions when it comes to money, it might help to take another look at your budget. Perhaps you'll be able to convince yourself that the money you delegate for personal use is accounted for and therefore meant to be used guilt-free. Having your own spending money for personal items may also help eliminate this guilt. I've mentioned this before, but I guess I'll say it one more time: Discuss money guilt with your mate. Who knows, he might be feeling the same way whenever he shells out cash for toys or stereo equipment. And I'm betting that you didn't get hitched to a man who'd want to deny you things that make you happy, regardless of the cost. Divulging all your feelings about money may prevent them from swirling around madly in your head.

taxing matrimony

There are two main issues that you and your mate should consider before celebrating (or dreading, as the case may be) your first April 15 as a married couple. The first issue is the proverbial marriage penalty, which basically means that upon getting hitched you'll likely pay more tax than you would if you and your partner earned the same respective amounts and were unhitched.

This issue, though, is a bit deceptive. It typically holds true only if you and your husband are making about the same amount of money because it pushes you into a higher tax bracket when you combine incomes. If one of you is unemployed or earning significantly less than your partner (as was the case when the current tax code was designed and women, who typically worked at home for no wages, were listed as dependents on their husband's filings), you won't incur the penalty. In fact, you'll experience the opposite: a decrease in annual income tax. Note: Congress recently attempted to remedy this problem. According to recent reports, spouses may see higher standard deductions, and married couples may get a more favorable tax calculation in 2005. Tax laws change every year and with every D.C. administration, though, so don't hold your breath.

To help offset additional money owed in April, courtesy of the marriage penalty, you and your husband should fill out new W-4 forms soon after you return from your honeymoon. Indicate your new "married" status (and your new last name, if you choose to change it) and then reevaluate your current withholdings. If both of you are working and earning about the same amount, you should increase your withholdings according to the W-4's worksheet recommendations (which are highly confusing and somewhat of a wild guess—calculations aside). Of course, when you increase your withholdings, you'll be bringing home less money per paycheck, but at least you won't owe Uncle Sam an alarming sum come April.

The second issue you'll want to consider is whether to file jointly or separately. Many couples—particularly those in which one spouse earns most or all of the income—file joint tax returns, because there are some tax benefits to doing so (lower rates, for instance). Filing separately, on the other hand, may make sense if both partners earn income but have separate deductions, such as when one partner has large medical expenses that wouldn't qualify as deductions in the higher combined income. For many couples, though, the tax return will be the same regardless of which way they file, so one way to approach the issue is to figure out both options and then go with the filing status that offers a lower tax (if one does, that is).

In a separate filing, you and your mate will file your taxes individually, using the "married (filing separately)" tax rates provided by the IRS. In a joint filing, your separate incomes and other financial details, such as how much money each of you has already given the IRS through individual withholdings, are combined on one tax return. You'll use the "married (filing jointly)" tax rates to determine your tax bite.

As when you were single, both filing statuses yield the same outcome: If you owe money, you'll send in a check; if you get a big fat refund, it's time to reevaluate your W-4s. Financial advisers say it's better to owe a little bit than receive a huge refund in April, since theoretically you could be making all sorts of profitable investments with that money rather than letting it sit with the IRS all year long, earning no interest. One last note on taxes: Since tax laws change every year, I highly recommend that you and your husband seek help from a tax consultant for your first filing as a married couple. This is especially advisable if you or your partner has tricky tax issues concerning trusts, capital gains or losses, and the like. Certified public accountants, enrolled agents, and tax attorneys (for the big questions) can fill you in on all the latest tax laws and possible perks, as well as advise you on other personal tax-related matters you may be concerned about.

financial security
(and other legal details)

As you and your mate discuss all things financial, here are a few final important items worth getting on the table.

insurance

You and your husband must have **health insurance**—at a bare minimum, enough to cover an emergency, in the event a car wreck or similar catastrophe strikes. That way, the last thing your partner has to deal with while you're recovering is paying off medical bills—and vice versa. Likewise, marriage is a good time to investigate **life insurance** and **disability insurance**, especially if you and your husband have children, a mortgage, or other serious debt (in many states, personal and joint debt are automatically transferred to your spouse upon death). Life and disability insurance offer financial protection in the event one of you is no longer able to bring an income into the home. Since many companies provide group insurance rates for these policies, first find out if you're already getting coverage from your employer (if you're like me, you've ignored all those insurance-related memos from Human Resources in the past). Then consider whether you need more coverage. Typically, you'll want five to seven times your annual salary, depending on your particular financial situation.

wills

You and your partner should write wills once you're married, especially if you have children or complicated personal finances. Without a will, state law (not your relatives) will determine how your property is divided upon your death.

And if you have children, a judge (not your surviving spouse) determines who gets to raise them. In many states, community property automatically goes to the remaining spouse, but personal assets are split between your spouse and any surviving relatives. Typically, there are associated fees and the process is slow, so it's wise to determine these matters yourself. If you and your husband don't have many assets, a handwritten will (called a holograph) might suffice, but check out your state's specifications for holographs first (http://www.nolo.com is an excellent reference for all legal matters). Also consider writing a **living will**. This legal document will give you the opportunity to express your desire for life-sustaining medical treatment (or not) in the event you become incapacitated.

power of attorney

The following legal documents serve to appoint someone (most likely your spouse) to handle all financial and medical decisions in the event you become incapacitated. A **durable power of attorney for finances** would enable your spouse to make financial decisions for you. (While some states allow spouses to manage each other's joint finances in these circumstances, many do not give spouses the capacity to manage each other's separate financial affairs, such as 401(k) investments or a private checking or credit card account.) Likewise, a **durable power of attorney for health care** would enable your spouse to make all medical decisions for you if you can't make them yourself, including whether or not to take you off life support (God forbid your spouse should ever have to make that decision). Unlike a living will, which only expresses your wishes, leaving the ultimate decisions up to your doctor, a durable power of attorney for health care gives your spouse legal means to make final decisions.

pre-nups and post-nups

Finally, these legal documents are relationship agreements that determine, among other things, who gets what in the event of a divorce. Many states consider all money and property acquired during marriage to be jointly owned. In these states, without a pre- or post-nuptial agreement, a divorce court judge could divide all assets earned during (and sometimes before) marriage fifty-fifty. That's one reason couples consider them. Another is if one partner has children from a previous relationship and wants to ensure that his or her premarital assets, and possibly his or her marital earnings, too, stay with the children rather than the ex if their marriage were to dissolve. Because the premise of a pre-nup is typically based on the possibility of divorce, these legal documents often brew passionate, hurtful questions in a relationship. If one of you wishes to have one and the other doesn't, I suggest you both look into premarital counseling. A professional can help you wade through all your emotions and concerns.

$\mathcal{G}$hosts from the past

Bear with me for a moment during my Academy Award–winning tribute to the clan members of my darling husband. I adore my in-laws. They are liberal, inquisitive, political, hilarious, and an altogether (there are many of them) unintimidating bloodline. Even better, they like to do the same kinds of things I do, such as cook neo-Californian-type foods that might well shame Martha Stewart back into her pre–celebrity days. And they enjoy hiking even when the weather is questionable. Getting together with them is an anticipated event. I know this is not true for every bride. I got lucky.

Why the ominous title of this chapter then? Well, because so many newlyweds have Issues (note the capital I) with their in-laws. The Issues aren't always as apparent as (true story) having your mother-in-law-to-be and all her friends boycott your wedding in protest of her son's choice in bride. Or as apparent as (another true story) having your mother and fiancé blow up at each other the day before your wedding because Mom's meddling is *stressing out the bride*. In fact, the Issues are often subtle, insidious, and virtually untraceable to their familial roots. Take the Issue of chore delegation. You and your mate's expectations of who does what around the house can often be traced back to how each of you witnessed the marital division of labor when you were growing up, but we'll talk more about that later on in this chapter.

Of course, the issues (note the lowercase i) aren't always Issues. Many of us experience relatively benign quirks and adjustments during that first year in which we are formally accepted into our husband's clan and our own family members make way for the new permanent addition of our husband into their lives. Maybe your family doesn't always get your husband's jokes. Or, worse, your husband doesn't laugh at theirs! Such adjustments often create awkward moments or even sources of confusion as to how to relate to one another.

There's an old adage that goes something like this: When you marry, you also crawl into bed with your husband's parents. I believe I've truly bastardized that old saw (I tend to do that), so I'll cut to the chase: Your husband *is* his parents, and you *are* yours (to some extent). Let's discuss the finer points of what you may expect among family members—his and yours—during the first year that you're hitched.

the hearty welcome

First, the good news: Many family members make an uncharacteristic effort to pull themselves together and be on their best behavior throughout the engagement, wedding festivities, and even first year of marriage, when everyone is still trying to figure each other out, if not impress. "After marriage, parents on both sides go through the process of investing in the couple and accepting the couple, because they are a keeper," notes family therapist Virginia Morgan Scott, of Santa Cruz, California. "It's a process, not a line they step over. In-laws go through their own honeymoon phase, too."

During this twinkling time, you may find yourself

amazed at how generous and hospitable your family is in welcoming your choice in life partner (and his family) into their homes and hearts. Some women even feel a prick of family pride they had buried since they began their quest for independence from Mom and Dad. Likewise, your husband's family may be operating on an exceptionally warm frequency during all the wedding prep, parties, and postnuptial gatherings. Bonding is often at its best during this optimistic time of change.

As families are merged, many newlyweds notice their relationships evolving. Maya, 32, of Portland, Oregon, says her father changed the most in her family. When she and her mate first started living together, Maya recalls, her dad wasn't too interested in getting to know him. Case in point: Dad was in town, and they went to meet him at a conference, where he, oddly, didn't introduce her mate to one of his colleagues. When Maya said something, her dad responded, "Oh, yeah, the boyfriend." Her mate was furious at the time, she says, but now he and her dad are great friends; her dad slaps her husband on the back and jokes around whenever they all get together.

Mandy, 32, of San Francisco, California, has also noticed a shift in her husband's family's reception. She says she feels more official—as if her new family is proud to introduce her to their friends. The acceptance has been so warm, in fact, that her only issue with in-laws is finding time to spend with them, especially around the holidays. By the way, where you and your husband spend the various religious or other family-gathering traditions that your respective clans observe is one of the greatest challenges of marriage. Not only will you and your mate likely get pressure from both sets of parents to spend Thanksgiving or Passover with them, but each of you will probably have your own nostalgic longings to be back home with your kinfolk and all their traditions (wacky and dysfunctional as they may be) during these times. We'll tackle the holiday issue in just a bit. For now, there's one more thing worth discussing during the initial welcome into the family: becoming a daughter-in-law.

What is this new role you're undertaking? To be honest, I can't really say since the role varies from woman to woman, family to family. Some of you won't notice much of a change in the way you interact with your in-laws now that you've become their daughter by marriage. Other women find themselves becoming an increasingly supportive and active member in their husband's family's lives—and that doesn't just mean sending them birthday presents when your husband forgets to (something I wouldn't recommend because it excuses your husband's negligence and places his familial obligations and considerations on your shoulders). Typically, the role of daughter-in-law defines itself over time, especially as your mate's parents age and the two of you begin to take on more of the responsibility for their care and well-being.

Deborah, 30, of Santa Cruz, California, found her role being defined when her husband's father grew terminally ill. His family is passive about obtaining information, Deborah explains, and they weren't getting the right kind of medical advice from their doctor. So she stepped in. After making phone calls and getting the doctor to explain what was going on with her father-in-law's health, she was able to function as the translator between family and hospital. All the while she made it clear to her in-laws that she was only there to help; if she started crossing lines they weren't comfortable with, she needed them to tell her. The family was, in turn, overwhelmingly appreciative.

Muriel, 30, of Portland, Oregon, says that her role, both to her and her husband's delight, has become one of friend to the women in his clan. It wasn't always that way (details in a minute), but after one weekend away with her husband's mom and three half-sisters, the five women have been dearly bonded ever since. During that trip they talked about difficult things—one of the sisters was having marital problems, for instance. Now the women look to each other for support. Muriel also makes a point of calling her husband's grandmother frequently to chat, simply because she loves the woman (and tells her so, too).

the culture clash (or when you just don't click)

Muriel's bonding success was mentioned above, but according to her, the relationship with her in-laws got off to a rough start primarily because she has such a different lifestyle from them. This became quite apparent the first Christmas she and her husband spent at their home. Even though his parents knew that the couple didn't eat meat, there was nothing in the house for them to eat that holiday season except processed soups. The whole event was awkward and rife with hurt feelings on both sides.

The fact is, many newlyweds experience a culture clash of sorts when it comes to getting to know their in-laws. Even though you may have always dreamed of palling around with your mother-in-law, sharing recipes and makeup and righting all wrongs from your own mother-daughter debacles during your sordid teenage years, you may find that cursory small talk and an occasional phone call or visit is as close as you will ever get (or want, for that matter). Take Nina, 30, of San Francisco, California, who grew up on welfare in East Los Angeles. Her husband spent his childhood in a wealthy, protected suburb of Columbus, Ohio. Nina admits she has the mouth of a sailor and concentrates hard on not cussing when she's around her in-laws. Once, "darn" slipped out, and her mother-in-law freaked. Nina says she's a hugger, but her in-laws are so Waspy that she never knows how to act around them. As a result, she always feels a little on guard in their presence.

Chloe, 26, of Santa Barbara, California, also felt a culture clash when she was first married. She's from a surfer town and was raised by a single mother. Her husband's parents live in a gated community—their house is the only one on the block. It took her about a year and a half before she felt comfortable around her in-laws, she says. The more time they spend with her in-laws, the closer she becomes. She no longer feels as if she has to dress up just to go over and hang out. The process involved getting to know their quirks, she says. She also notes that her in-laws were very involved when she and her husband entered the market for a house, and those interactions helped them get to know each other better.

Getting over the culture shock generally takes time and patience. And an open mind, says Helen, 33, of Washington, D.C. She has become very close to her mother-in-law—even to the point of talking to her about her mate, though "never in a bitchy sort of way, but more about who he is and why, and how she's dealt with different aspects of his personality," she says. While Helen admits she has the in-law connection pretty easy, she points out that it's important for women to realize that in-laws are your extended family, and for that reason it's in your best interest to find *something* you like about them. Nobody's perfect, she says, so you shouldn't hold your in-laws up to the same standards as, say, your own parents. Or anyone else you admire (or don't), for that matter.

The more you get to know your in-laws, the more likely you'll find opportunities to appease the culture clash—or at least contain it so you're able to visit a couple of times a year without dashing to the nearest Buddhist monastery afterward to rinse your mind of all the evil thoughts inspired by your visit. Molly, 31, of Philadelphia, Pennsylvania, recalls the moment the ice broke between her and her father-in-law. He is the kind of man who has opinions about *everything* and always has to have the last word, qualities that have always irritated her. About a year and a half into her marriage, a rap song came out that had famous quotes from history. The family happened to be sitting around the table at dinner one evening when the song came on the radio. One of Molly's siblings-in-law asked where the "ask not what your country can do for you" reference originated.

Molly's father-in-law was quick to attribute that quote to President John F. Kennedy but then went off on a soliloquy about how great the '50s were, saying how it was the best time the country had ever experienced. Molly, who had always toned down her liberal political views in front of her in-laws, had finally had enough and said, "Yes, if you were a white male." Then she went off on her own soliloquy about the racial inequality and women's rights issues that polluted the decade. Her father-in-law was completely taken by surprise, she says. But it also seemed to her as though he respected her speaking out. Since then she's been able to be more herself around her in-laws, which has helped break down the tension, subtle as it may have been in the first place.

Barbara, 30, of Staten Island, New York, and her husband experienced the cultural divide on each end of the in-law spectrum. His parents, for starters, are extremely loud, she says. In the mornings they all gathered around the breakfast table, gabbing and debating stories in the paper. Her clan, on the other hand, is silent and mellow at dawn. When the couple first visited her side of the family, Barbara's husband wasn't even sure he was allowed to talk in the morning, everyone was so quiet. But compared to the clashes she has experienced in becoming part of her husband's family, the volume issue is a non-issue.

"My mother-in-law is very opinionated—she'll say things about my hair being too long or my eyebrows too thick. She loves me and wants me to 'look pretty,'" Barbara says. It drives her nuts. Gradually, she has come to accept her mother-in-law's quirks and move on. Her father-in-law (for privacy's sake, let's call him Mitch Black) was the harder nut to crack. The first time she met him, he made her cry because he insinuated that she didn't know her own mother very well. Nothing is private in her husband's family, and opinions fly out of the mouth. Her ice-breaking moment was on her wedding day when she asked her father-in-law if she could now call him by his first name instead of Mr. Black. When he told her bluntly that he was Mr. Black to her, she responded by saying, "Okay, Mitch," which made him laugh hysterically and finally broke the ice. (And, yes, she still calls him by his first name.)

Even Nina had an ice-breaking moment with her Waspy mother-in-law, who gave her etiquette books for the wedding. It happened right before the big day, actually, when in a moment of panic Nina dashed to her future in-laws' hotel room and begged them to help her drag her fiancé off the golf course so he could help her write their wedding vows. Mother-in-law took her son to task, calling him on his cell phone and telling him to get to their room right away because his bride was crying and there was work to be done. *Voilà!* Vows were written, and the situation brought the two women, different as they are, a smidgen closer.

ghosts from the past

It should be no surprise to hear that your parents are going to be playing a minor role in your marriage. After all, you've already turned into your mother by now, haven't you? In most marriages the parental unit intrudes upon you and your mate mentally, not physically (although some newly-weds are unfortunate enough to experience both). Mentally speaking, you and your husband will be bombarded by phantom messages about marriage that are based on child-hood impressions formed by your respective parents' mar-riages and, let's be real here, their divorces. Unfortunately, the mental invasions, unlike the physical ones, are unavoid-able. You can't take the key away from your past, can you?

The reason I call these flashes from the past "ghosts" rather than a more sanguine word such as "vision" or "inspi-ration" is that they often (unless you've been to therapy) lead to narrow-mindedness, which is the bane of marriage. What's more, these ghosts are stubborn and like to get their way. Unless you and your mate are influenced by the same childhood images of marriage, including such mundane issues as how a couple should manage the household expenses and when they should open Christmas presents (eve or morning of?) and how to argue constructively, these ghosts will compete for running the show. Family therapists say that many newlyweds subconsciously try to recreate in their own marriage the family and home life they wish they had experienced growing up. That also explains the appearance of ghosts during the first year of matrimony, when you and your husband are creating a new life together.

Dara, 27, of Tampa, Florida, was well aware of the influence her parents' marriage had on hers. So much so that she purposely did things differently once she got married. "I grew up in a household where my dad didn't clean or do the dishes, and I didn't want to be in that kind of situation. For a while I was terrified that I was going to be the maid," she says. So when she and her husband got hitched, she intentionally wouldn't do such things as iron her husband's clothes or have dinner on the table every night when he got home from work (she works at home) so he wouldn't start expecting those things from her.

Allison, 27, of Dallas, Texas, has a ghost from her past, too. When she was in middle school (the most hellish of all times, I'll take the liberty of adding for dramatic effect), her father's company went bankrupt. Her family had major problems with money because of that, and as a result it scares her to think of her and her husband running out of money or mismanaging their funds. When her husband recently started up his own company, Allison was terrified. Even though she supported her husband's dream and their joint decision for him to go for it, she was fearful because of her own childhood experience with bankruptcy.

Another common parent-inspired ghost that many newlyweds grapple with has to do with their views on the very institution of marriage. Alexis, 27, of San Antonio, Texas, comes from a family of divorce. Her views of marriage are tainted by memories of cheating and bitter disputes. For her, divorce is an option when things go wrong. Her husband, on the other hand, comes from a family in which his parents have been married for thirty years. "He has a strong faith in marriage," says Alexis. "His parents fight like hell. Months, even years, go by when they're not happy. But eventually there is a peak, and things are okay between them. Divorce doesn't come to my husband's mind when we get in fights—marriage is something you stick with." Alexis knows that her background puts her at risk of running away when things get bad, but she admits that's cowardly. And her husband is helping her be less afraid of bad times between them.

In fact, challenging your ghosts is critical during the first year of marriage when you and your mate are merging lives and forming the foundation on which to approach, manage, and maintain your marriage for years to come. It's never easy to look back at your past and try to determine how your upbringing might be warping your current process of living, but it's important to at least consider the possibility. The key thing to keep in mind here is that ghosts never disappear on their own. They must be exorcised (best achieved through therapy or by reading self-help books) and replaced by new lifestyle visions (best determined jointly by you and your mate, often by role-modeling your own marriage after those of family and friends whose marriages you admire).

the out-laws

In the best of worlds your in-laws are irresistible. In the real world they're an affable lot and no more than occasionally irritating to be around. But in some cases they are nothing less than a pill that must be swallowed whole (or, in the worst-case scenario, spit out).

Take the in-laws of Kathleen, 27, of Portland, Oregon. She suspects that the men in her husband's family do not respect women, and that really puts her off. Her father-in-law, for instance, cheated on his wife. Her sister-in-law had an abusive husband. When Kathleen became pregnant and decided she wanted to start going to church, her brother-in-law pulled her husband aside for a secret family conference, and tried to talk him out of the Catholic church they were thinking of joining. And that's just one example of her brother-in-law's trying to push his views on them, she says.

Jamie, 28, of Newport Beach, California, has also had problems, primarily with her sister-in-law who insisted that her toddler accompany her other child, who was the flower girl, in their wedding. Jamie felt a two-year-old was too young to participate in such a formal event and didn't want the stress of anticipating a toddler meltdown during his walk down the aisle. When Jamie said no thanks to the suggestion, her sister-in-law threatened to boycott their wedding. If both kids weren't going to be part of the show, then none of them would show up. Eventually, Jamie's future parents-in-law helped mediate the conflict, and everyone attended, but there's been tension ever since.

In fact, Jamie says that was only the beginning of problems with her husband's sister, who became a big issue during her first year of marriage. In another incident the sister-in-law accused Jamie of putting her father-in-law's health at risk because Jamie accepted his offer to pick her up at the airport when she went to visit. How do you deal with a nut who is also your husband's sibling? That is the question.

Candace, 34, of New York City, advises this: Lower your expectations, be civil to one another, and then move on. She, too, has had issues with her sister-in-law, who she believes is overly protective of her two brothers (one of whom Candace married) and not accustomed to sharing their affections with another woman. At their rehearsal dinner, which the sister-in-law had arranged, she placed a big picture of her two brothers in the middle of the guests-of-honor's table. Suspiciously absent was any image of Candace; but her mother, at the last minute, graciously supplied the missing photo of the couple whom everyone was there to celebrate.

managing the in-laws

Obviously not all in-laws are as criminal as those mentioned above. Hopefully, yours aren't. But if they are, there is one very important thing to keep in mind: *They are the ones who have serious problems, not you!* Not only do such people lack critical skills in fostering interpersonal relationships, but they are just plain wrong, not to mention rude, to treat you like an escapee from San Quentin. If your husband doesn't stand up for you or attempt to reprimand his clan members for unacceptable behavior directed toward his choice of a lifelong partner, then your husband, too, has some serious issues. Translation: He has never separated from his clan and has no clue as to how to set up boundaries between his life and theirs. In the event you are faced with such conundrums, here are a few tips for making the in-law interactions civil or at least bearable.

draw a line in the sand

If in-laws (or your own parents, as the case may be) are sticking their noses into your private affairs or knocking down your or your husband's self-esteem, it's time to reestablish the boundaries. So learned Alicia, 34, of Kailua, Hawaii. When she first got married, Alicia was excited about becoming part of her husband's close-knit family—

until her mother-in-law's domineering manner became too much to handle. When the couple extended a simple invitation for her to come over for dinner, the event became a long-drawn-out, stressful ordeal that was entirely dictated by the frantic energy of her mother-in-law, who was supposed to be their guest but insisted on a three-course meal.

Then came the used furniture—first a teeny broken TV, then a sagging chair—"gifts" from said mother-in-law (who really was trying to get rid of the stuff). This was a particularly sore point for Alicia because her mother-in-law's gifts to her other children and their spouses were always brand-new, making her feel that they were the dumping ground couple. Needless to say, both of these issues would have been bearable had her mother-in-law not continuously made fun of Alicia's eating habits. Tofu had become the family joke.

Gradually, Alicia began setting boundaries. She stopped going to every family party, which always made her anxious, and let her husband go on his own. She finally told her mother-in-law that they didn't want anymore used furniture, they were happy with their household the way it was. The tension Alicia once felt toward her mother-in-law slowly lifted. "At first I was worried that I would offend her if I didn't go to every party she threw or refused her hand-me-downs," says Alicia. "But it turned out to be no big deal. If she was hurt, she dealt with it. In-laws will adjust to you, just as you adjust to them."

Marguerite, 32, of Indianapolis, Indiana, also had to set up boundaries for her mother-in-law, who is 74 and very dependent on her only child, Marguerite's husband. "She has a lot of health concerns, lives in senior housing, and is an incredibly high-maintenance personality," says Marguerite. "Nothing is good enough for her. She pushes.

She'll say that we never spend enough time with her. It's been a huge challenge for us as a couple." As a result, Marguerite and her husband had to establish some boundaries, something her husband had never done on his own. "I had to be hard-ass," Marguerite says. "My approach was to decide what was fair. We need to feel like decent human beings, so we talked about what seems appropriate—visiting her once a week or twice. I've tried to encourage my husband to think about our needs as well as hers, so we're not in the position of letting his mother tell us what to do."

Warning: As you begin to establish boundaries, you may meet resistance from your own folks, who aren't used to living by your rules. Erin, 27, of San Francisco, California, admits her dad is overbearing, and that has been hard for her as she and her husband attempt to make their own decisions. "My dad has always been intimately involved in the details of my life. He is my only parent and has been my financial adviser and professional mentor. Even after my marriage he wants to give me advice on everything from investing to buying life insurance. He gets upset when I don't tell him things that my husband and I are doing," she says. "This drives my husband crazy, so I'm learning what I can and cannot reveal to my dad about our personal life."

Jane, 31, of Fairfax, California, has also met resistance from her mother as she and her husband have begun to establish boundaries, particularly those related to where they spend their holidays (a huge issue for many couples, as I mentioned before). "I'm very close to my family and have always spent the big holidays with them," says Jane. "Now that I have two families, my mom has started pressuring us to commit our time to them. She pouts and pushes, but we've told her that we'll be alternating holidays between families. I don't put up with her moods, and she's learning not to be so insistent."

By the way, alternating years for the big family holidays seems to be the way to go on this contentious issue. Another way to approach the where-to-spend Thanksgiving/Hanukkah/Christmas/Kwanza/Winter Solstice debate is to decide which family has a stronger affinity for the various holidays in question and offer your presence accordingly. My husband's family's premium annual celebration is Thanksgiving, so we tend to roast turkey with them. My family, on the other hand, goes all out on Christmas. We have at least three different family parties on Christmas Day and a separate celebration on Christmas Eve, so my husband and I try to travel back to Dallas, my old stomping grounds, in late December. Mindy, 25, of Somerset, New Jersey, and her husband have solved their dispute over this issue in this way: She spends part of Christmas with his family, then flies by herself to her folks' home to spend the rest of the holiday with them.

Jamie has also had to establish boundaries with her own family, whom she and her husband are equally close to. During one visit back home she overheard her mother complaining about her to her husband, who sat there and said nothing. (Her husband, in his defense, felt terrible about the situation but didn't know how to respond to his mother-in-law's rant at the time.) When Jamie walked in on them, demanding to know why her mother was bad-mouthing her, her mom tried to blow it off as a big misunderstanding. She and her mom didn't talk for over a day, until Jamie brought up the incident again. She told her mother that she was sorry if she felt she couldn't confront her about some issue personally, but that talking behind her back to her husband was destructive to her marriage and hurtful, and it could really backfire on her someday. Her mother, surprisingly, agreed that she was right. Since then her mother has not overstepped her boundaries again.

Boundaries are critical for maintaining a healthy marriage because they help everyone involved understand this simple fact: In marriage your primary allegiance is to your spouse, not your family. Ann, 28, of San Francisco, California, clarified this with her husband soon after they tied the knot. "We had to have a serious talk about his family," she says. "My husband is very close to his mother and sisters. I asked him, 'Do you realize that you'd have to choose me over your mom and sisters if we were all in a crisis at the same time?'" The situation had never occurred to him, Ann says, and he had to really think about it. It was important for Ann to know that his allegiance was to her and that by marrying her he was essentially shifting his primary commitments from his family of birth to his family of choice.

don't try to mend fences

If your husband is distant, cold, or even estranged from his family, it is not your job to try to "fix" things between the parties in question. This is not an uncommon scenario, notes family therapist Virginia Morgan Scott. "Women are often more relationship oriented and start to mend fences. That almost always blows up," she says. "If a guy warns his wife not to be nice to his mother, she should listen to him. That's his solution, perhaps, to dealing with a socially demanding mother."

If you do attempt to right all past wrongs and bring your husband closer to his family, you may find yourself in the middle of a nasty war. Although Alicia never went to war, she did get a taste of this when she and her husband first got hitched (this was before the used furniture and tofu insult incidents). "At first I was really encouraging the idea of spending more time with my husband's family. He didn't want to. But I felt obligated to do things with them, and I was excited about the whole in-law thing. After a while, I pulled back. I realized that I was overstepping boundaries that he had set up."

get to know them better

If the in-law blues are dragging your marriage down, one option is to spend more time with them. While this may not seem like the best option available, it can't hurt to try. It has slowly been smoothing the edge between Paula's husband and mother. "My husband has problems with my mother because she's so judgmental," says Paula, 31, of Spokane, Washington. "When we got engaged, my mother was very upset because she felt she didn't know my fiancé very well. She didn't want me to move away from southern California, and she's very mistrustful. She made me cry about my decision to get married, and that infuriated my husband." Since they've been married, though, Paula says her husband has made a huge effort to repair the wounds. He frequently chats with her mom on the phone so she'll have an opportunity to get to know him better. Slowly, the ice is melting and relations are improving.

turn them into grandparents

I'm not suggesting that you should ever consider having a baby just to get on the in-laws' good side; however, I would like to make this observation: Many women say that having a baby was the sole act that brought them closer to their in-laws. (It goes without saying that having a baby will also change your relationship with your husband!)

One woman I interviewed said that her baby greatly improved her relations with her mother-in-law—perhaps because there was a third party to focus on. Also, she notes, "There's something about producing a child that creates a bond between women, and that really cuts out a lot of riff-raff." Of course, presenting your in-laws with their progeny may also ignite a whole new slew of in-law issues (unso-licited advice being one of them). But that is another book that I'll save for later.

$\mathcal{O}$n becoming a "smug married"

I'm a devoted fan of Bridget Jones, who through talented author Helen Fielding best articulated the great divide between married and single women in her infamous diary. Jones called her hitched girlfriends "smug married" as she recounted the wretched horrors of couples-based dinner parties and rogue inquiries therein about her singleton sex life.

Although I don't consider myself smug (at least in the marital sense), I can relate to the lack of relatability between hitched girls and those who are uninitiated in marital stress (but not liberated from the relationship uncertainty of a single girl's lifestyle, let's be clear). The great divide is only one of the subtle social changes many of you will experience after tying the knot. What follows are some of the more common dynamics that may await your social life following the wedding.

a status shift

Marriage may change a girl's social standing in two diametrically opposite ways. Conventional society (a group into which, for convenience's sake, I will lump older people, many married couples, and corporate America) may treat you with more respect after marriage, as though you have finally "arrived" at your place in the common order of society.

Amber, 30, of San Francisco, California, felt the shift occur as early as her wedding, where one of her hitched girlfriends hugged her and whispered in her ear, "Welcome to the club!"

Amber has noticed that she gets more respect as a married woman and that people take her more seriously. She points out, for example, that when she's making plane reservations, the ticketing people are nicer to her if she says that she's traveling with her husband. Marguerite, 32, of Indianapolis, Indiana, has also noticed an increased acceptance and a social advantage due to marriage. It still astounds her that she can get personal information about her husband over the phone—health care insurance details, airplane ticketing information—just by saying that she is his wife. And for those of you who live in parts of the country that disregard women in subtle or overt ways, having a husband gives you the added cachet of male authority (if only by extension). Mention to your mechanic what your husband thinks is wrong with the car, and you'll likely get straightforward service. Infuriating, but true.

Allison, 27, of Dallas, Texas, also feels that marriage has given her added maturity in the eyes of others, particularly her coworkers. Young for the position she holds at the advertising firm where she works, Allison says that marriage has enabled her to relate to colleagues above her as well as her clients, who are typically older. "I've always been self-conscious about being so much younger than my coworkers," she says. "Marriage has helped me with my career because I have more things to talk about with clients and coworkers. I can relate to them on things like bills and buying a house."

Then there's the other rank of social order, including people younger than you and many of your single peers.

This group of people may look at you as though you are out of your mind for committing yourself to another person for the rest of your life. I might also add that if you are marrying at a young age (such as before you turn 25), you may also get this disturbed attitude from older peers like me and confidants who worry that you just might be a tad too inexperienced in relationships to take the marital vow. (But if you are younger than 25, go ahead and prove me wrong. I'll be rooting for you!)

Muriel, 30, of Portland, Oregon, said that she was nervous about telling her friends five years ago that she and her boyfriend had gotten engaged. She was afraid they would react as though it was a bad thing. Indeed, when she relayed the news, her friends' jaws dropped. Muriel and her mate were the first couple in their group of friends to get married, and the very concept of matrimony stunned the circle—most likely because, theorizes Muriel, it made everyone reevaluate their own relationships, wondering if they, too, should be taking the next step. Since she's gotten hitched, she says, people look at her differently—as though she's now older, more mature, a real adult.

Isabelle, 29, of Chicago, Illinois, noticed a similar adverse response when she got hitched. "Strangers I met at parties or through work all had the same reaction when they learned I had a husband—complete and utter astonishment," she recalls. "They seemed unable or unwilling to grasp the fact that a 27-year-old would willfully commit to marriage." Isabelle found this reaction especially common among single men, who suddenly started acting very bizarre around her, such as abruptly ending the conversation as soon as they found out she wasn't single. She attributes this reaction to two possible causes: One, she threatened them because she was capable of snagging a man and getting him to marry her, and two, she was no longer a conquest. As a married woman she was off-limits and therefore of no interest to them.

Alicia, 34, of Kailua, Hawaii, also noticed a change in the way her guy friends acted around her soon after she got engaged. Basically, she stopped hearing from them. At first hurt by their blow-off, she decided to take the rebuff as a sign of change and simply move on. Still, she missed the fun, flirty friendships she once had with them. Obviously, not all guys get hives when they confront married or engaged women, but some do, so don't be shocked if you experience such social reactions from your male peers.

your new best friend

In addition to the altered view that society may have of you now that you're hitched, many married women talk of the commonly observed shift in confidants. Instead of turning to their best girlfriend at the end of the day to discuss the nightmare neighbors' barking dog, married women will instead share all the intimate, mundane, as well as fascinating details of daily living with their husband, who is generally more accessible and (for the most part) interested in daily drama than is a friend—if only because he's often directly affected by it. Chloe, 26, of Santa Barbara, California, says she doesn't crave going out with friends as much anymore because now she has her best friend (her husband) with her all the time. She admits that she doesn't get lonely as much as she used to, so she doesn't need to see her friends as often as she did prior to marriage. Because of that, she says she has fewer friends since she tied the knot.

The new best friend feature, brought to you by marriage, predicts another common social phenomenon: Your allegiance will likely shift, too. The most important person in your life will no longer be a parent, sibling, or best friend, but instead will be your husband, the person to whom you have pledged a lifelong commitment of support and fidelity. He is the one to whom you will likely offer the vast majority of your personal reserve of energy, compassion, listening capacity, advice, and passion. This is because you and your mate will be sharing a household, money, and family—three of the most stressful aspects of life. They often become even more stressful when you try to share the responsibilities of them with another person who has his own way of dealing with them. Because your livelihood and future are so enmeshed with that of your mate, nurturing this relationship becomes a primary goal, whether your subconscious is aware of that or not.

Another impact that the allegiance to your soul mate may have on your friendships is a decreased degree of openness. Many married women find themselves much less candid when speaking about their relationship to family and friends—even their former confidantes. In the past when you weren't getting enough sex, all your closest girlfriends were likely to know about it (and, of course, offer suggestions for improved frequency). Or when your boyfriend was being a jerk, you may have called three or four wise girlfriends to get perspective and advice on what to do. For many, that changes once you become hitched.

Avery, 33, of New York, New York, says that her friends don't know everything that's going on with her and her husband anymore. If she and her mate argue, she no longer rushes to the phone to process it with her friends, as she would have with boyfriends in the past or before she and her husband got engaged. Sometimes, she says, the increased privacy factor makes her feel lonely because she doesn't know who to turn to when she and her husband aren't feeling connected. At the same time, though, she says that blabbing about their personal life to others feels like a betrayal.

Jamie, 28, of Newport Beach, California, also doesn't want to reveal relationship problems to her friends or family now that she's married. She attributes her increased discretion to not wanting friends to know that her relationship occasionally has problems, an admittance that would not only be embarrassing but also feel as though she was failing at marriage. She also points out that telling others about little problems or disagreements could give them the wrong impression of her marriage. If she calls one friend in the aftermath of a heated argument with her mate, her friend may wrongly suspect that her marriage is having some serious setbacks, when in fact it is not. While Jamie may easily forget her phone rant in a day or so, her friend probably won't. That's another reason that she has become more discreet.

Determining how much of their relationship they want to share with others is a work in progress for many newlywed women. On the one hand, they don't want to distance their close friends from what's going on in their life (more on that next). On the other hand, they don't want to betray their husband's confidence. What many women find is that after the initial adjustment to marriage, they're able to reestablish a new type of intimacy with friends, one that's reminiscent of the share-all connections of yore but is not quite as open as when they were single. In most cases, with some effort on both sides of the friendship, these relationships will evolve into a new form of intimacy. Evolution is a very important concept to grasp when it comes to friendships post-wedding.

single girls, inc.

Speaking of evolution, earlier in this chapter I mentioned the following social phenomenon: Marriage often prompts a Darwinian divide between single girlfriends and those who are hitched (a.k.a. the "smug married"). Upon tying the knot there is an unspoken requirement to relinquish your membership in Single Girls, Inc., and your friendships with its active members will often become compromised. Based on my many interviews on the matter, here are some of the most common reasons that the great divide occurs:

1. **YOU JUST CAN'T RELATE.** Not only will you begin to have a lower tolerance for the travails of dating (i.e., "Should I call him or not?"), but your single girlfriends will also develop an aversion to your increasingly domesticated lifestyle ("You guys rented a movie *again?*"). Also, Avery points out, single girlfriends don't always comprehend how married relationships are different from theirs. For instance, they might not understand that fighting in a marriage is very different from having an argument with a boyfriend. "A husband is forever," she says, "so marital fights have different implications. They must be worked out."

   The inability to relate on certain matters is particularly true if your friendships with said single chicks were built on the common goal of finding a mate. If the female bonding was born in bars where scamming on potential mates was the primary activity, and if that connection never developed into deeper friendships through other activities, such as traveling together or going on hikes or rock climbing, then the friendships will likely fizzle soon after marriage. Of course, if you attempt to expand the bond into other areas, the fizzle won't likely occur, but if you and your single girlfriends can't move away from bachelor-analysis and on-the-prowl activities that bonded you in the first place, then consider yourself fore-warned: The friendship is in grave danger.

2. YOUR LIFESTYLES ARE INCREASINGLY AT ODDS. Marriage may change your lifestyle pretty drastically. For instance, you may start sharing money goals with someone else, which could affect how much cash you spend when going out with friends. Also, you're sharing a home with your mate, which means phone calls at 1 A.M. (or even 10 P.M.) might not be acceptable any-more. It also means that your home is less private for girl-gathering and for girl-gabbing on the phone.

Candace, 34, of New York, New York, refuses to answer the phone after 10 P.M. "That's my quiet time," she says. "It's important for my husband and me to have that time together. It's what we need to do to make our relationship work." Her single friends don't always grasp that concept, though, and she admits that it's frustrating. For that reason she's become closer to other married friends, who are going through similar life changes and understand, for instance, that she can't talk on the phone for half an hour if her hus-band has had a bad day and wants comfort and attention from *his* best friend.

The increased stress on a relationship that marriage often brings may also demand an increase in downtime spent with your mate. For many married women the only downtime they have available in their hectic and overscheduled lives is on the weekends. As a result, friendships often lose priority for Friday and Saturday nights (which is generally prime time for gathering among single girls). Not only does this make it harder to keep friendships evolving, but it also leads to resentment, which takes me to the next common cause of friction.

3. HURT FEELINGS. Both sides of the friendship divide risk hurting each other's feelings due to the changes brought by marriage. Single girlfriends may feel abandoned by their married friends, who often don't take into consideration how lonely the single lifestyle can be—especially on the weekends and at the end of the day when conversation with an old friend is truly appreciated. For some of these single women their friend's marriage brings anxiety about their own lifestyle choices, making it harder to be around wedded friends (especially if the hitched couple is the type that indulges in overtly annoying PDA).

Married women, on the other hand, may feel left out of the loop among their single gal pals. Avery, for instance, says that some of her friends have stopped calling her at home since she got married, perhaps because they are afraid of bugging her and her husband. Single friends may also feel inhibited about leaving voice-mail messages on their married girlfriends' machines because they know their friend's husband might also hear them. Or the voice mail message might even be in the husband's voice, which further emphasizes the loss of privacy, among other things, that forces a change in the friendship.

Jill, 25, of Kansas City, Missouri, says that her single friends seem to have forgotten that she can get together with them without her husband in tow. When her four closest girlfriends decided to go away for Memorial Day weekend, they assumed she wouldn't be able to go and didn't include her in the planning. She was finally invited after everyone had already gotten plane tickets. Ann, 28, of San Francisco, California, also noticed this subtle exclusion from her pack of single girlfriends. Her friends started up what they call Martha Stewart Night, in which they do crafty projects together. Ann doesn't always get invited.

4. **LESS TIME FOR ONE-ON-ONE SOCIALIZING.** Another thing that Single Girls, Inc., often forgets is that many married women double their social network after tying the knot. Not only is a hitched woman gaining a husband, but she's also gaining formal acceptance into her mate's tribe of friends and family. Certainly this acceptance was going on during the initial courtship and the months leading up to the wedding, but once you get married, the desire to further these relationships often becomes more intense, because you're going to be involved with them for the rest of your life. When a hitched girl makes an effort to socialize with her newly inherited circle, she'll have less time available for maintaining her own group of friends.

On a similar note, a hitched chick also may have an increased desire to further solidify her mate's connection to her own social circle because it makes socializing all the more convenient when you can bring everyone together at once. As a result, a married woman may increasingly invite her mate to get-togethers with friends. It makes sense, after all, to get these connections brewing so that a couple can enjoy their social time with each set of friends. However, these all-inclusive gatherings often compromise one-on-one time with girlfriends, which sometimes encourages the great divide.

5. **LACK OF DIRECTION.** Finally, one of the biggest culprits of the split between single and married friends is a lack of discussion on how marriage might affect their friendships. Hopefully, marriage won't change the deep-seated bond between you and your premarriage friends, especially your closest girlfriends. Those bonds are so important and sacred to the female soul, they're critical to protect. Both married and single women need to figure out ways to maintain the female bond despite the life changes that make it harder to keep.

Since you, the newlywed, are the one who is changing the code of ethics between you and your girlfriends by tying the knot, it's important for you to initiate these discussions. Start by deciding which friendships are worth nurturing at this point in your life and concentrate on those relationships. Friendships that are not healthy or growing in a positive way are better downsized to the status of acquaintance. (Hope, 37, of New York City, put the downsizing tactic frankly: "That B-list of friends is out.")

Next, let the friends you do want to keep know how much you value their companionship and how important they are in your life, even if you aren't quite as available to them as you once were. Make honest efforts to check in with these friends at least once a week—through a quick phone call or email—at a minimum. Then make a point to see them one-on-one in addition to meeting up with them, husband in tow. During your private bonding, be sure to do things that will help your friendship grow—ideally activities that are fun and challenging and active. Weekends away with the girls are great for this type of bonding. If you and your friends only reconnect by doing drinks after work or the occasional dinner here and there, those friendships will begin to feel stifling and boring. Consequently, they won't evolve at the pace of everything else going on in the rest of your life.

merging circles

For a marriage to remain social—which it needs to do in order to feel connected to most of the world, unless you and your mate are both intensely introverted, God help you—you and your husband must merge social lives to some degree. I say to *some* degree because I think it's very important to maintain your own private bonds with friends as well. Merging, however, is important for two reasons. One, if you don't attempt to get to know each other's friends by spending time with them as a couple, you may begin to lose these friends because you won't have enough time to maintain the one-on-one closeness with all the disparate aquaintances each of you has. This is especially true once you and your mate start a family. Two, it's critical to expose your relationship to the energies of your closest confidants, who are valuable sources of inspiration, excitement, and entertainment. If you don't, your own relationship will begin to feel isolated and boring.

Merging groups of friends isn't always easy, though. Unless you and your mate were part of the same group of friends when the initial sparks flew or you've been together for so long that you can't quite recall whose friends were whose in the beginning, you may find the process difficult— especially if you don't like some of your husband's pals. Or if your husband doesn't care for *your* friends.

Erin, 27, of San Francisco, California, had trouble with one of her husband's friends, whom she didn't like at all. She says they talked about it, and her husband explained why he liked this friend and what he could and couldn't expect from him. She decided to handle the situation by lowering her expectations rather than ask her husband to stop hanging out with him. Helen, 33, of Washington, D.C., had a similar experience. She says that both she and her husband had certain friends whom the other saw in a different light, specifically a bad influence on the other. They encouraged each other to really look at their friendships to see if certain people were draining them. They told each other their gut feelings about some friends, then left it up to the other to decide if he or she wanted to keep that friendship or not.

Alicia, too, has dealt with this issue; her husband didn't

like one of her closest friends. She handled the situation by attempting to explain what she saw in the friend at stake. She also made a point of telling her husband that she understood why he didn't like this woman, but nevertheless she saw certain qualities in her that made her want to continue the friendship. Now she sees her friend primarily on her own. But she also brings the two together now and then, though not for extended periods of time.

Sometimes time is all that is needed to break the ice when merging friends. Alexis, 27, of San Antonio, Texas, for instance, had a hard time becoming a member of her husband's circle of friends, a tightly knit group rich with private jokes and several years' worth of stories and adventures under their belts. Initially the circle was very protective of her husband when she first started dating him, wanting only the best for him. Although she's not shy, Alexis says she gets nervous when she's overwhelmed, and the pressure of wanting to fit in (but feeling like an outsider) made it harder for her to establish connections. Still, she forced herself to spend time with her husband's friends, even going out with them when her mate was out of town. Gradually, the barriers broke down, and she has begun to develop her own personal relationships with some of them.

socializing for two

Making connections, establishing a history, and sharing experiences that spawn stories and jokes and trust is really what it's all about when it comes to friendships in marriage. For many reasons—moving to a new city to be with a spouse or finding yourself in an increasingly incompatible lifestyle with old friends are two primary ones—you and your mate may discover that you are lacking in social interaction. Since emailing and weekly phone calls to girlfriends who live across the country can only make you feel partly connected, now's a good time to review the basics in making new friends, particularly when you are a couple.

But first I might as well mention that for a married woman a quest for new friends has two parts: (1) find girlfriends, single and married, with whom you enjoy doing things on your own (this is essential for maintaining your sense of autonomy, which I've mentioned several times in this book), and (2) meet other couples that both you and your mate can relate to. Dara, 27, of Tampa, Florida, points out how hard it is to find couple friends that you both really like. Inevitably, she says, both of you will end up liking only half of the couple. Or you'll find a couple you both like, but they have kids, so you're not always on the same page. Basically, making new friends takes time and initiative.

Once you do find friends you like as a couple, though, it's important to expose the fledgling friendship to activities in which companionship, trust, and fun can flourish. This is typically not achieved through the proverbial dinner party, social activity of choice for many couples. While the dinner party may serve for convenience (Molly, 31, of Philadelphia, Pennsylvania, has discovered that gathering her disparate group of friends all together now and then for a dinner party is the only way she can keep in touch with all of them), its function is one of maintenance rather than evolution. Keep that in mind when you're trying to establish new friendships. Evolution of a friendship, on the other hand, requires action. Organize a group ski trip or gathering at the local beach or park—anything that doesn't exclusively revolve around a stagnant dinner plate. Not only will these relationships have a better chance to grow, but you'll also have much more fun.

*t*he six gospels of marriage

About five months into our first year of marriage, my husband and I found a fixer-upper we could afford (sort of) in the Bay Area. We had been looking for a house since we returned from our honeymoon and had already made two offers on two places. We'd lost both due to the dastardly bidding wars that were infiltrating the local real estate scene, making homeownership virtually impossible for those of us who don't have trust funds. The day before we braced ourselves to make a bid that would put us in debt for the next thirty years, the owners pulled the house off the market, and our dreams were dashed—until I had the brilliant idea (if I do say so myself) of making an offer anyway and seeing what the owners might say. To our utter astonishment, our offer was accepted, *sans* gruesome bidding war, and we found ourselves trying out the new title of home owner.

Never mind that the 1914 craftsman bungalow was sliding down a hill, sat half a mile away from the Hayward fault (which seismologists say is just about due for a rumble), and had questionable foundation issues that revealed themselves in a prominent hump on the living room floor. And never mind that the abandoned house next door was a fire hazard and home to a pack of raccoons that would soon drive us crazy by tearing up the little plot of Kentucky bluegrass, which we planted in our cabana-styled backyard soon after our arrival. The house was a testament to our future. It was ours. We loved it.

We still do. In fact, we adore our home—slanted floors and all. We cherish it so much that we vowed to restore it to its original integrity (that's architectural speak for the following: stripping wood, refinishing the floors, painting, and leveling what we've endearingly nicknamed "the hump," to mention just a few items on our renovation to-do list). Soon after we moved in, we began our mission. First there was a leak in the toilet, which my engineer husband, after several discouraging attempts (I'll spare you the crude details), successfully disassembled, fixed, then put back together again, *fait accompli*. Then there was the random patch of wood on the dining room floor that had never been stained, which we promptly sanded, refinished, and sealed with polyurethane to near perfection (at least to the casual observer). We've recently begun the heinous task of stripping the multilayers of lead-based paint from all the doors and window trims and built-ins. When I'm not sitting at my desk writing, I'm donning a respirator and scraping off eighty years' worth of layers upon layers of paint—stark white, pale green, mustard yellow, creamed coffee.

I'm sure you're wondering right about now what this has to do with marriage. Honest, I'm not going off on a tangent. Buying and fixing up a house has *everything* to do with marriage. It has forced my husband and me to compromise like we never have before. There are so many opinions on what to do with the house and how to go about doing it. We've been faced with money stress and power struggles (as in "My method of painting the ceiling is far more efficient than yours!") unlike any other conflicts our relationship has endured. In retrospect, planning our reception was a piece of wedding cake compared to deciding which light sconce looks better in the living room or trying to convince my husband, much as I adore him and his impeccable taste, that his stereo equipment looks weird inside the antique built-in bookcases that frame our brick fireplace. No matter how ideal your marriage, as I like to think of mine, conflict inevitably intrudes upon the bliss now and then.

Someone once told me that there are two things in life that will really test your marriage: having a baby and buying a house. I'm so thankful that we did the house bit first because it has given our marriage a glimpse into the way we deal with passionate disagreements and stress. (Who knew a girl could get so riled up about the proper method of pre-serving first-growth Douglas fir?) More important, it's given us valuable practice in coping with conflict. Plus, it has given us the chance to work together on a common cause, which has been as equally rewarding as challenging. Though I'm not naive enough to believe that co-owning a home has in any way prepared us for parenthood (I was an editor at *Parenting* magazine for many years, so I'm well aware of the stresses that a newborn brings to a marriage, especially when you add sleep deprivation into the mix), I do believe it has made our relationship stronger, more resilient to setbacks, and altogether empowered.

I guess what I'm trying to say, long-winded though I may be, is that all marriages go through their own unique enrichment processes, the blueprints of which most often appear during the first year of marriage when so much adjustment is taking place. There are valuable lessons in this adaptation process, difficult as it may seem at the time. I call these lessons the gospels of marriage, and there are six, in particular, that you and your mate might be wise to strive for during your first year of marriage—especially during those rocky moments that every couple must endure to reach the higher, more enlightened form of love.

Memorize the gospels now, girl, then check back on this chapter now and then when your relationship feels overbearing. I can't promise that the gospels will cure all your marital woes, but they sure will make the rough times easier to deal with. Oddly enough, the gospels all begin with the letter *F.* Don't ask me for an auspicious explanation of the F connection. Let's just say that it's an alliterative fluke.

gospel #1: flexibility

While it should come as no surprise that flexibility is one of the requisite gospels of marriage, the *degree* of flexibility will certainly come as a shocker. And you and your partner will need to master this flexibility while adapting to each other's quirks and daily rhythms and unanticipated dramas (such as, say, when one of you gets laid off, forcing your coveted vacation fund to serve as supplemental income instead of a month's holiday in Rome). Without flexibility, you and your mate set yourselves up for power struggles, bitter battles for control over each other, which ultimately corrode those bonds that brought the two of you together in the first place. A relationship is nothing if it is not flexible. Actually, I take that back. It is *something*—it's broken!

Flexibility comes in two parts: mental and emotional. Of course, there's physical flexibility, too, and that will do wonders for your relationship in the bedroom, but let's stick with the two that are more difficult to achieve. (For physical flexibility, try yoga or a ten-minute stretching session after each workout.)

Mental flexibility is typically achieved through two means: admission and adaptation. By admission I mean owning up to the fact that you don't always know best—

even if you secretly believe that you are superior and more evolved than your mate. Admit that your husband's views on such matters as long-term goals and financial planning are compelling and worth considering (even if they conflict with yours). And admit that his method of tackling such shared tasks as laundry, dishes, or the bills is no less menacing than yours is; it's just different.

Admission of these differences typically opens you up to adaptation, which is the simple act of trying new ways of doing things and attempting to see the world from your husband's point of view. Adapting to small changes will help prepare you and your mate for the bigger ones that may be beyond your control down the road, such as when you decide you want to get an MBA and must ask your professor husband to quit his teaching position in Atlanta and move with you to Manhattan so you can go to NYU, your first choice. Or when your husband discovers he has a genetic disease that will require a complete overhaul of your current lifestyles, including a standing Saturday commitment to physical therapy and the added pressure of never losing your current health care policy, which serves both of you. When combined, admission and adaptation will grant you greater mental flexibility, which in turn will strengthen your relationship, which requires so much more compromise (and compassion) once a lifelong commitment enters the picture.

Emotional flexibility is equally important to your marriage. What I mean by this is the ability to experience the full range of human emotions within eye- and earshot of your chosen mate. It also means learning how to respond (or, when the case calls for it, not respond) to your mate's expression of his entire spectrum of emotions. For both of you that means being able to move fluidly from anger, such as when your husband for the nth time leaves his boxers crumbled up on the floor next to the dirty clothes hamper (by the way, what *is* that with men?), to forgiveness, such as when he sheepishly tosses his dirty clothes into the hamper after you remind him that you both agreed this is where they go upon being discarded from the body. It also means being able to glide from fervent frustration over such vital disagreements as how to organize all your shared legal and financial documents to hilarity that something as frivolous as organizational differences are the bane of your marital existence. To remain fully engaged in a passionate relationship, both partners must be fully engaged with all their emotions as well as be free to express them when they feel the need. If one or both of you gets rigidly stuck in one emotional framework, say anger or apathy, denying all other emotions, from joy to fear to pleasure to adoration, you will never evolve as a couple (or a human being, for that matter, but let's stick to the topic of marital enlightenment).

Becoming emotionally flexible requires two things: learning to express your emotions and learning how to listen without judgment or commentary to those of your partner. Getting in touch with your own emotions and then having the courage to reveal them, full monty, to your mate is a hard and sometimes frightening challenge, especially if you never learned how to do so as a bachelorette. If you have trouble in this area, I suggest therapy. Hey, I endured three years of it during my twenties, and it really helped me get in touch with my pre- and postadolescent angst, not to mention all the disappointments I experienced during my early experimentations in career and love. But enough about me.

Getting in touch with your partner's emotions is equally challenging, especially if your mate has trouble keeping you informed about everything that's going on inside. Remember, your husband has a responsibility to let himself be known to you. If he can't reveal all aspects of his emotional wiring, he, too, might do well with some professional guidance.

One thing you can do to help stretch your partner's emotional reach, though, is to be receptive to all the inner workings of his mind. In other words, listen to your partner—*really* listen. That means taking in his stories and emotional reactions to them without criticizing, interrupting, commenting, or offering him advice (one of the toughest challenges for me, since giving advice is, well, my business). Giving your partner a nonjudgmental platform on which to vent his emotional state will not only allow you a front-row seat into his mind and heart but will also give him the opportunity to see how well you can be trusted to receive his full display of emotions. There is nothing like emotional flexibility to bring a husband and wife closer together.

gospel #2: friendship

Pardon me if the friendship factor seems obvious, but some couples let the drudgery of daily living wear down the critical bond of camaraderie, which many experts contend is the essential ingredient to lifelong love. If you're an avid reader of women's magazines, you've surely stumbled across the name John Gottman, Ph.D., the relationship guru of the Pacific Northwest whose infamous "Love Lab" in Seattle has scientifically studied couples for nearly two decades, attempting to discern, among other things, what makes a marriage last.

In his book *The Seven Principles for Making Marriage Work*, Gottman narrows marital success down to one common denominator: friendship. According to his studies, even couples who fight in a manner that might make a marriage counselor cringe behind her legal pad, if they have an underlying friendship that's thicker than blood, they'll probably be one of the few couples who end up celebrating their fiftieth wedding anniversary. Yes, even if they must battle such discouraging elements as insulting in-laws, careers that keep them apart from each other for weeks, and a combined salary that forces them to shop for home décor at Target instead of the Ralph Lauren home design center at Bloomingdale's.

Let's take a look at what exactly thicker-than-blood–type friendship entails for a married couple. For starters, true friendship begins with mutual respect. This, unfortunately, cannot be contrived—you either have it or you don't. If you never have had respect for your partner (or vice versa), then deep down you believe that you're superior. You're out of luck, girl. Why the heck would you marry someone you don't respect? So that you can always feel as though you're in control? I don't mean to be crude or overly cynical, but if that's the case, I smell divorce court.

If, however, you have a deep-seated respect and admiration for your partner but occasionally forget to reveal your reverence and awe, then you're in luck. All you need is a reminder that paying attention to all the reasons you fell in love with your partner, *and then frequently telling and showing your partner how much you revere and respect him,* is critical for maintaining a rich, enduring relationship. Indeed, if in the thick of an argument over whose turn it is to wash the dishes you can remind yourself that your husband is a decent human being who loves animals and babies (or whatever qualities attracted you to him in the first place), you may have more respect for his reasoning as to why he needs to skip dish duty that night. (Perhaps it was because he saw a dog nip a baby on the way home from work, and it really rocked his worldview?) Whatever the excuse, respect can go a long way toward helping you and your mate cope with the myriad unromantic doldrums of communal living.

Another element of friendship maintenance that some of us unwittingly stray away from during marriage is keeping tabs on each other's independent lives outside of the marital bond. Of course, if you and your mate are equally extroverted, you probably don't suffer from tuning each other out at the end of the day. But those of us who are introverted at heart need to remember the importance of casual chit-chat, the kind you eagerly indulged in during your courtship when you gabbed on the phone with each other for hours, talking about nothing and everything.

Much as you may prefer to check out of the real world at the end of an exhausting day and curl up on the sofa to escape into a novel or HBO, I highly recommend that you and your mate make a habit of keeping each other posted on each other's daily events. From the new projects you acquired at work to the gossip of coworkers and mutual friends, to your suddenly realized ambitions, frustrations, successes, and failures, it is important to keep each other intricately involved in your separate lives. Connectivity is the root of a lifelong friendship. So is fun.

Not only does fun add levity to a marriage, but it also serves as a fabulous stress releaser. If your idea of fun involves exercise, then all the better. Jackie, 30, of El Dorado Hills, California, goes on an hour's walk with her mate every evening during the witching hour as well as hikes on weekends. It's a double dose of rejuvenation.

Fun does not always have to be organized, such as

going on a rock-climbing venture with your mate and climbing friends every weekend. Nor does it have to be exceptionally involved, such as organizing a group of friends to see a play that just opened or planning a special weekend getaway at the nearest spa (although these activities certainly are worth planning every so often because they help all types of relationships grow—especially if you and your mate and joint pals share a passion for such things as film festivals, traveling, or outdoor adventure). Fun can simply involve trying out that restaurant all your friends are talking about, hitting your favorite watering hole every Thursday evening after hours as you did when you were first dating, going to see a matinee on a whim, or wasting an entire evening doing nothing but telling each other silly jokes and looking at old photos of when you first started dating.

gospel #3: faith

There are three kinds of faith worth acquiring in marriage: faith in yourself (also known as self-respect), faith in your partner, and faith in the relationship itself. If you're religious, you'll also want to strive for faith in whatever god or goddess you worship, of course, since in many religions marriage is a divine act. But since I'm no clergyperson (and definitely no saint), let's stick to the secular.

Having faith in yourself—or, put another way, having strong self-esteem—is essential to a happy, lifelong relationship because it frees you from neediness, a deadweight in any relationship. Neediness prevents one from giving. Without a hearty dose of self-respect, self-love, and all the other "self" words that don't carry negative connotations, you could fall into the trap of relying entirely on your husband for a sense of worthiness, which is a tough order for any human to fill. Women (and men, too) who rely solely on their partner's approval or judgment in order to feel good about themselves or to feel whole ultimately put themselves in a psychologically dangerous predicament, because their entire sense of worth will be dependent on someone else. To be able to give fully and equally within a relationship, which all married individuals must strive to do, each partner must first take responsibility for his or her own happiness.

You may remember that in Chapter 4 I wrote that many hitched women say marriage has increased their self-esteem. I fall into that category, mainly because I feel so accepted by my husband. Naturally, having a strong supporter who cares about all the minuscule details of your life, as a good husband should, will help boost your confidence. Don't get me wrong—there's nothing wrong with that. But a boost is really all you should be looking for in your mate. The root of your confidence should come from within.

If you lack self-esteem, therapy (yes, again!) might be calling you. If you're not taking care of yourself healthwise (as in getting daily exercise and relaxation, maintaining your friendship connections, and eating healthy foods), then start improving those areas, too. Ditto with your spirituality, which is closely linked to self-worth, I believe. Treating yourself with dignity and worth breeds high self-esteem. Consider faith in yourself as critical to marriage as ample closet space.

Equally vital within this gospel is having faith in your partner. This is because in marriage you will likely begin to see new dimensions of your husband that either escaped your notice during the blinding phases of courtship (when we all censor certain parts of ourselves) or are new personality developments. These changes may first appear disconcerting to you because they're different from what you bargained for at the altar. However, change is healthy (not to mention unavoidable) for both members of a lifelong relationship.

If your husband changes in dangerous ways—becomes mentally or physically abusive or develops addictions that put you or your family in harm's way or prevent intimacy—I suggest you immediately find a safe haven and seek therapy (there it is again!) for starters. Otherwise, it's important to have faith that minor personality changes will lead to your relationship's growth, not its demise. Remember Muriel, 30, of Portland, Oregon, whose husband started collecting orchids as a hobby and now has two thousand in the greenhouse he built in their backyard? Muriel admits her husband's infatuation with orchids scares her because they cost a lot of money to maintain. But she's supporting his dream of starting up a side business and clinging to her faith in him. "Trusting him is key, but it's hard," she says. "Sometimes he's wrong about things. But I try to stay in the present moment and trust."

So keep the faith when your mate decides he wants to start up his own business or longs to be a stay-at-home daddy instead of a corporate earner. If you started out with a core respect and admiration for your mate (the friendship factor I mentioned earlier), then trust will help you get through your doubts and fears, of which I guarantee there will be many.

Last but definitely not least, it's important to have faith in your relationship. By that I mean trusting that your relationship is unique and right on course, regardless of how it compares to your best friend's marriage or to Hollywood's latest romantic comedies (many of which might make your own marriage seem substandard, inadequate, or even boring if you get sucked into the fantasy). If you absorb one thing from this chapter, please remember this refrain: Screw the Joneses! I don't mean this literally (unless you have *that* kind of marriage). What I mean is simply this: Avoid measuring your marriage against anyone else's. Instead, have confidence that your relationship is evolving the way that makes sense for you and your mate (and your unique personalities, dreams, and lifestyles). Have faith that whatever you're doing and however you're doing it are right for you.

gospel #4: fantasy

Fantasy is as important to lifelong love as faith. Without actively imagining what your joint future may hold, the reality of daily living—clogged sinks, screwy bosses, car payments, and all—could get the best of you and your mate.

Remember how fantastical those final months leading up to your wedding day were? At the time they were hell, I'm sure, but if you're reading this well into your first year of marriage, you've likely forgotten the mundane details and the unexpected fights you had with your mate, and can only recall the excitement, the charmed synchronicity, and the glowing expectation of what was to come. Here's a secret: The wedding day fantasy that you and your mate held on to as you planned the elaborate event is probably what got you through those stressful times, and that is an important lesson to take with you through the rest of your marriage. Dreaming is essential.

I recommend that you and your mate regularly indulge in fantasy—where you want to spend your next vacation, what kind of dream house you want to buy and how you want to decorate it, what your children will look like and what you'll name them, what you'd do if you won the lottery, as well as where you're going to take your grandchildren (yes, grandchildren!) to celebrate their graduation from elementary school. How does that song from *South Pacific* go? "You got to have a dream/If you don't have a dream/How you gonna have a dream come true?" My sentiment exactly.

Fantasy does not have to exist in conversation alone. I also recommend that you and your mate regularly indulge in fantasy as a form of relaxation and escape. To put it more directly so there's no confusion on the matter, take a vacation at least twice a year. If you can save your paid time off and the necessary cash to fund two trips, one of which is at least a week long (the other can be a long weekend), far removed from any reminder of your normal life, then promise me you'll do that. And no fair trying to squeeze in time with family during this vacation. This escape is all about you and your relationship.

You'll need the R&R to rejuvenate you, to relieve stress that has naturally built up over time between you and your coconspirator in life. You'll need it so that you can forget about who forgot to clean the bathroom or who has an annoying habit of leaving mail scattered around the house. You'll need it so that you can fall back in love with your mate and make uninhibited, unhurried love whenever the mood stirs. Marriage without a dose of fantasy is a somber affair indeed.

gospel #5: fecundity

By fecundity I don't mean to suggest that you and your mate have lots and lots of babies (although that may be one expression of the fecundity I *am* talking about). What I'm implying in this gospel is that a creative, intellectually productive marriage—one in which the participants share a higher purpose in life than, say, paying off a mortgage or retiring young—is a soulful marriage. Without fecundity, whether that takes the form of growing a garden together or joining the local synagogue or becoming politically involved within your community, your relationship is at risk of losing passion and connectivity over time.

A higher purpose for many couples, of course, is raising a family. And, honestly, that may be one of the highest purposes there is in a long-term relationship. After all, without the parental unit devoting time and wisdom and love to raising the next generation to populate (and hopefully preserve) our world, would there be purpose to anything anyone does? I'm certainly no philosopher, but I'd have to say no.

Until babies invade your love nest (and so that you'll have something to keep your marital bonds evolving while your babies are transmogrifying into angst-ridden teens) or if you're nonparent types, you and your mate should regularly engage in activities that bond your spirits. That may take the form of volunteering for a cause you both believe in, cultivating an herb garden, or taking a class together to learn more about something that ignites passions in both of you. Or it could take a more spiritual turn by your joining a religious organization that revs your spirits. At any rate, the goal is to find a common calling in life that you and your mate can both relate to and grow from. This will sustain, strengthen, and enrich your marriage unlike any other gospel because sharing any creative, inspiring passion with your life partner will help connect you at the core.

Just so you don't start overanalyzing your relationship, I'll share with you a confession: I don't know what the mission of my marriage is right now, either. I have a few vague notions: We want to raise a family, we both care about pre-serving the environment, and we both feel most in awe when confronting nature in its rawest state—on a cliff overlooking the ocean, on top of a windswept mountain, hiking in a grove of ancient redwoods. Eventually our mission will make itself clear. Yours will, too. In the meantime, indulge in activities that give you and your husband clues. Look for opportunities that you and your mate can spiritually grow from. And strive for joint missions that will help sustain a soulful union for years and years to come.

gospel #6: farsightedness

The final gospel has to do with vision. Specifically, farsightedness. Biologically speaking, seeing distant objects clearly and near objects nebulously can wreak havoc in one's life (especially if your profession relies on keen vision, as it would for a surgeon or copy editor). But in marriage, farsightedness has the opposite effect. In fact, it is a bonus in marriage because it helps you and your mate keep perspective as you make your way through life's stresses and throwbacks. What's more, farsightedness keeps you focused on future goals and your joint mission—the big picture—so that you don't get weighed down by minor obstructions along the way.

I don't mean to sound like Pollyanna here. I'm not suggesting that you overlook your marriage's failings when they arise (and they will). Nor am I suggesting that you don't periodically analyze your life and strive to make appropriate changes when needed. But I am suggesting that you make a conscious choice whenever you're faced with myopic setbacks and ask yourself if, for example, your husband's lack of enthusiasm for vacuuming the house on a weekly basis *really* matters in the big scheme of things. Surely a compromise can be made. Is his infatuation with buying every electronic gadget that pops up as an advertisement in his email really worth getting your underwear in a curl? Certainly a budget can be drafted and used as a guide for your mate's enthusiastic spending habits.

We've all heard the saying, "Choose your battles." Excuse the cliché, but this is exceptionally wise advice for those of us practicing the gospel of farsightedness. Instead of wasting precious energy on petty arguments and negative thoughts about your husband or your marriage, focus on the positive, creative aspects of your relationship. This vision will get you through some of the rough times that all married couples face. And it will get you through those times with a lot less agony and stress than you might otherwise experience. Farsightedness involves a determination to make your marriage last for the long haul. With a farsighted vision, I guarantee you'll have a pretty good shot at living happily ever after.

TEN

$\mathcal{H}$appy anniversary!

Lawrence and I celebrated our first anniversary over a long weekend of cross-country skiing in the Sierras. The trip was reminiscent of our first weekend away together five years earlier when we had ventured on skis into the backcountry of Sequoia National Forest, a few hours' drive inland from San Francisco.

Whenever we look back at our first weekend away together, we have to laugh. The snow was icy and dangerous. We had forgotten to bring water. By the end of the first day, we were eating snow to stave off dehydration and throwing our ski poles out of frustration from falling. I had unexpectedly gotten my period during the day's ventures (I'll spare you the details of how I coped!), and Lawrence was feverish and vomiting from dehydration. Talk about trying to impress each other! The trip would have been a complete disaster had we not been so blinded by the thrill of our budding relationship. It still ranks high on my list of favorite adventures.

This time around, though, we approached the backcountry with a little more foresight and sophistication. For starters, we brought plenty of water and food. In the preceding years we also became a little more adept at handling cross-country skis. As luck would have it, the snow conditions were ideal. Lawrence even booked a room at a Scandinavian-style B & B that had a wood-burning sauna and a cozy restaurant with an extraordinary menu.

To this mountain hideaway we brought a bottle of pinot noir we had saved for months from one of our trips up north to the Russian River wine region during the year. Curled up next to a crackling fire after a day on the mountain, we recounted all the events of our first year hitched. We relived our New Zealand honeymoon, our weekends away, our professional accomplishments, and our house purchase (and getting into the groove of fixing it up). Then there were all the babies—eight in total—who had graced so many of our friends and families. (Warning: As soon as you tie the knot, all your couple friends will start having babies, making you wonder if it's the time to start a family too.)

On the evening of our anniversary, we borrowed an idea from my married sister and decided to create a photo album—the first in a planned lifelong series—reflecting all the events that happened during year one. Sorting through the year's worth of photos we brought with us to the mountain that weekend, we chose the most representative images and placed them in the album. Then we talked about our hopes and dreams for year two.

Our relationship had grown exponentially since our first ski venture five years earlier. But the reality is that most of that growth happened during the year that just passed. It's an extraordinary time, year one of marriage. Filled with optimism, challenges, and endless compromises, it's a poignant time of growth in any relationship, a "once-in-a-life opportunity for your love and relationship to grow and spread like wildfire," says one of my hitched girlfriends.

I hope this book has given you some insight into the

private (and sometimes not so private) life of a hitched girl. Like all good things in life, marriage has its ups and downs. What I've hoped to show you is that the downs are normal and to be expected. After all, you're restructuring your entire life after tying the knot, and that can breed anxiety and confusion in even the most emotionally stable.

As you plan your first anniversary, I'd like to share a few suggestions for celebrating the end of year one. Of course, however you and your mate decide to honor the day is perfectly suited to the occasion, I'm sure. But those of us who have had a little experience in the area offer the following advice.

make resolutions

I have always loved making resolutions at the beginning of each year. As chance would have it, my wedding anniversary falls on January 6, which makes marital resolutions easy for me because resolutions are already on my mind. As you read in Chapter 9, one of the gospels of marriage is to dream feverishly and fervently about your future, and that's exactly what should be done here. What better time to fantasize about everything you'd like to accomplish with your mate in the coming year than on your anniversary, the day you're honoring the past, present, and future of your relationship?

Personally, resolutions give me a structure that helps me make decisions when I'm faced with choices during the new year. Whether or not I actually achieve them is beside the point. The object is for me and my mate to touch base with our goals and values, both of which will change throughout life. One of our resolutions for year two was to finish the renovation of our home (or at least do as much as we could on our limited budget). We also resolved to take one last hurrah adventure-vacation before attempting to start a family. I'll let you know how those went in my next book.

create traditions

Your first year of marriage is certainly not the beginning of the history between you and your mate, but it will likely be the start of many of your family traditions, such as how you'll celebrate the holidays now that you have proper kitchen equipment to throw a dinner party for family or friends, how you'll tell each other good-bye in the morning before work, and how you'll ease back into the homestead once your public lives are done at the end of each day. Likewise, your first anniversary will be setting the tone for future wedding anniversaries.

That's why I'm going to suggest that you and your mate spend extra time planning a very sacred and special way to welcome another year in your relationship. Sure, dinner out is a wonderful way to celebrate, but I suggest something even more meaningful. I already told you about creating an annual photo album, an idea I stole from my sister and her husband. You might also consider an annual viewing of your wedding video (saving it for a once-a-year screening will keep it special) or perhaps even reading each other's wedding vows as a reminder of what your relationship is really all about. Avery, 33, of New York, New York, and her husband kept a journal of their wedding and honeymoon. Each year on their anniversary they pull it out and relive the memories.

Since it's your first year, by all means drag that cake out

of the freezer (if you saved the top piece for the occasion) and invite your family and friends over for a special tasting. Don't fret if the cake has gone bad or is suffering from freezer burn. It doesn't mean a thing. (In fact, our bakery advised us against this tradition, citing bacterial concerns. Yuck!)

Finally, consider starting an annual observance to mark the day. For instance, vow to always take the day off from work and spend it together doing something both of you really love—skiing, kayaking, having a picnic at the park where you first picnicked together, revisiting the place where you tied the knot or got engaged. Physical, active celebrations are great not only for creating memories but also for helping you and your mate wind down after all the daily demands of work and maintaining the household. The physical unwinding will make it easier to relish the moment. And don't forget to bring a camera: These will be great pictures to kick off your photo album for year two.

make mad, passionate love

Do I even need to tell you this? Probably not, but I thought it'd be a lovely way to end the book. Making mad, passionate love is the heart and soul of marriage. Lovemaking is the surest road to intimacy, especially if you take the windy route whenever possible, and it's the straightest path to pleasure. So indulge. Happy anniversary!

*R*esources

The following books and Web sites are great sources of information for love and marriage.

Bach, David, *Smart Couples Finish Rich* (Broadway Books, 2001).

In-depth financial planning advice for couples that covers everything from establishing financial goals to balancing your retirement portfolios.

Corn, Laura, *101 Nights of Grrreat Sex* (Park Avenue Publishers, 1995).

———. *The Great American Sex Diet* (William Morrow, 2001).

Both books offer lively tips for enhancing monogamy.

Gottman, John, Ph.D., *The Seven Principles for Making Marriage Work* (Crown Publishing Group, 1999).

With sixteen years of research on marriage and divorce under his belt, Gottman reveals the key skills and personality qualities common among happily married couples.

Larson, Jeffry H., Ph.D., *Should We Stay Together?* (Jossey-Bass, 2000).

Dissects all the issues that marriage brings to the plate and offers practical advice for couples trying to decide if the time is right to tie the knot.

Maltz, Wendy, *Private Thoughts: Exploring the Power of Women's Sexual Fantasies* (New World Library, 2001)

Examines women's sexual fantasies and reveals the fascinating role they play in our sexuality.

Good Vibrations (http://www.goodvibes.com).

A clearinghouse for sex toys, sex education, and erotic and how-to books and videos—all for the sake of your (and your husband's) pleasure.

Nolo: Law for All (http://nolo.com).

Legal information you can't live without

Smart Marriages: The Coalition for Marriage, Family, and Couples Education (http://www.smartmarriages.com).

A clearinghouse to help couples find the information they need to strengthen their marriage and family. Includes a catalog of relationship courses that teach pro-marriage and relationship skills. A note about these courses: Many colleges and secondary schools offer classes that teach relationship skills. If you're affiliated with a religious organization, it may have its own version of faith-based marriage prep classes. For a secular approach, look for a course taught by a licensed marriage or family therapist, preferably one that's based on research, indicated by the following snappy little acronyms: PREP (prevention and relationship enhancement program), PAIRS (practical application of relationship skills), or RE (relationship enhancement).